My
Windows®
Phone 7

Brien Posey

Que®

800 East 96th Street,
Indianapolis, Indiana 46240 USA

My Windows® Phone 7

Copyright © 2012 by Pearson Education, Inc.

ISBN-13: 978-0-7897-4825-6
ISBN-10: 0-7897-4825-8

Library of Congress Cataloging-in-Publication Data is on file.

Printed in the United States of America

First Printing: December 2011

Trademarks

All terms mentioned in this book that are known to be trademarks or service marks have been appropriately capitalized. Que Publishing cannot attest to the accuracy of this information. Use of a term in this book should not be regarded as affecting the validity of any trademark or service mark.

Warning and Disclaimer

Every effort has been made to make this book as complete and as accurate as possible, but no warranty or fitness is implied. The information provided is on an "as is" basis. The author and the publisher shall have neither liability nor responsibility to any person or entity with respect to any loss or damages arising from the information contained in this book.

Bulk Sales

Que Publishing offers excellent discounts on this book when ordered in quantity for bulk purchases or special sales. For more information, please contact

U.S. Corporate and Government Sales

1-800-382-3419

corpsales@pearsontechgroup.com

For sales outside of the U.S., please contact

International Sales

international@pearson.com

EDITOR-IN-CHIEF
Greg Wiegand

ACQUISITIONS EDITOR
Loretta Yates

MANAGING EDITOR
Kristy Hart

PROJECT EDITOR
Andy Beaster

DEVELOPMENT EDITOR
Todd Brakke

COPY EDITOR
Language Logistics, LLC

SENIOR INDEXER
Cheryl Lenser

PROOFREADER
Dan Knott

TECHNICAL EDITOR
Troy Thompson

PUBLISHING COORDINATOR
Cindy Teeters

BOOK DESIGNER
Anne Jones

COMPOSITOR
Bronkella Publishing LLC

Contents at a Glance

Table of Contents

About the Author

Brien Posey is a seven-time Microsoft MVP with two decades of IT experience. Prior to becoming a freelance technical writer, Brien served as CIO for a national chain of hospitals and healthcare facilities. He has also worked as a network administrator for some of the nation's largest insurance companies and for the Department of Defense at Fort Knox.

Since going freelance in 2001, Brien has become a prolific technical author. He has published many thousands of articles and numerous books on a wide variety of IT topics (primarily focusing on enterprise networking). In addition to his writing, Brien has provided consulting services to clients all over the world and occasionally speaks at various IT conferences.

When Brien isn't busy writing, he enjoys traveling to exotic places around the world with his wife, Taz. Together they have visited more than 50 countries. In fact, a portion of this book was written during an expedition to Antarctica. Some of Brien's other personal interests include scuba diving, aviation, and shredding waves in his Cigarette boat.

Dedication

I would like to dedicate this book to my wife, Taz, for her love and support throughout my entire writing career.

Acknowledgments

First and foremost, I would like to thank my wife, Taz, for her patience and understanding while I was writing this book. Writing a book is a time-consuming process that unfortunately results in friends, family, and household chores being neglected. I feel fortunate to have a wife who has put up with my crazy writing schedule for the past 16 years and understands when I have to dedicate extra time to my writing.

I would also like to thank Loretta Yates for allowing me to write this book and for providing me with many other writing opportunities over the years. It is always a pleasure to work with Loretta, and her easy-going attitude helps to ease the stress involved in taking on a project like this one.

Finally, I want to thank Troy Thompson for doing the technical editing for yet another one of my books. I first met Troy back in the late 1990s when we both worked at Fort Knox (thanks again for helping me to pass my Exchange Server exam). Even though I left Fort Knox in the late '90s, Troy has remained one of my best friends and has helped me with numerous projects like this one. I sleep well at night knowing that Troy is hard at work trying to keep my mistakes from making it into print.

We Want to Hear from You!

As the reader of this book, *you* are our most important critic and commentator. We value your opinion and want to know what we're doing right, what we could do better, what areas you'd like to see us publish in, and any other words of wisdom you're willing to pass our way.

As an associate publisher for Que Publishing, I welcome your comments. You can email or write me directly to let me know what you did or didn't like about this book—as well as what we can do to make our books better.

Please note that I cannot help you with technical problems related to the topic of this book. We do have a User Services group, however, where I will forward specific technical questions related to the book.

When you write, please be sure to include this book's title and author as well as your name, email address, and phone number. I will carefully review your comments and share them with the author and editors who worked on the book.

Email: feedback@quepublishing.com

Mail: Greg Wiegand
Associate Publisher
Que Publishing
800 East 96th Street
Indianapolis, IN 46240 USA

Reader Services

Visit our website and register this book at quepublishing.com/register for convenient access to any updates, downloads, or errata that might be available for this book.

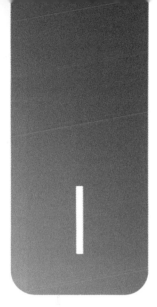

Introduction

As someone who has been working with Windows phones and other Windows Mobile devices for well over a decade, I am amazed by just how far the technology has come. Windows Phone 7 includes features that were absolutely unheard of in previous Windows Mobile operating systems, such as an integrated Zune, Xbox Live, and one-touch access to multiple email accounts.

As a way of helping you to better appreciate just how far Windows phones have come, I want to start out by giving you a brief history of the Windows Mobile operating system. After that, I talk about some of the most notable changes (both good and bad) that Microsoft has made in Windows Phone 7.

The History of Windows Mobile

Microsoft's first mobile operating system was Windows CE, which stood for Compact Edition. It was based on extremely stripped down Windows 95 code. In creating Windows CE, Microsoft removed the APIs for everything that wasn't absolutely critical so that they could make Windows small enough to run on a mobile device. Of course back then there were no Windows phones. The first Windows CE devices were little more than glorified PDAs.

Over the years, Windows CE has gone through quite an evolution. The picture that follows shows several Windows Mobile devices and, except for the Windows Phone 7 device, all of them were based on Windows CE code.

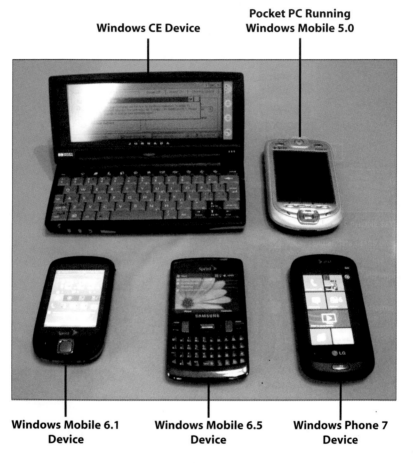

Windows CE Device

Pocket PC Running Windows Mobile 5.0

Windows Mobile 6.1 Device

Windows Mobile 6.5 Device

Windows Phone 7 Device

The device shown in the upper left corner of the figure is an HP Jornada, which runs Windows CE 2.0. The Jornada (which I purchased somewhere around the year 2000) functioned similarly to a mini laptop but couldn't run applications that were designed for desktop versions of Windows. The device was really quite extraordinary for the time period but ultimately never caught on because of its $1,000+ price tag. In case you are wondering, the thing that made this device so costly was that it was one of the first mobile devices to include a color screen.

The device in the upper right corner of the screen is a Pocket PC, which ran Windows Mobile 5 (otherwise known as Windows CE 5.0). In spite of the name change, Windows Mobile differed very little from earlier versions of Windows CE, except that it was designed to run on a cell phone such as this one (which I purchased sometime around 2004). This device isn't powered on because I accidentally destroyed it by jumping off my boat into the water while the device was in my pocket. Even so, you can see what the operating system looked like in the figure.

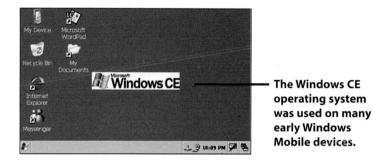

The Windows CE operating system was used on many early Windows Mobile devices.

The device in the lower left corner of the screen is running Windows Mobile 6.1. This device, which was from around 2007, is still based on the original Windows CE code. However, Microsoft kept extending the code base over the years. Windows Mobile 6.1 Professional was the first version of Windows Mobile to support domain enrollment and group policy usage.

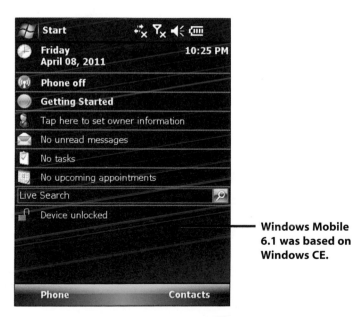

Windows Mobile 6.1 was based on Windows CE.

The device in the lower center portion of the figure is running Windows Mobile 6.5, which was the last Windows Mobile release prior to Windows Phone 7. Even though Windows Mobile devices have come equipped with touch screens for at least ten years, Windows Mobile 6.5 was the first edition to come with an interface that was specifically designed to make using the touch screen without the aid of a stylus practical. It also featured a greatly improved Web browser. Even so, the Windows Mobile 6.5 operating system was evolutionary and contained some code that dated back all the way to Windows CE.

Windows Mobile 6.5 was the version of Windows Mobile that was released just before Windows 7.

The device in the lower right corner of the screen is an LG Quantum running the Windows Phone 7 operating system. As I mentioned earlier, Microsoft did away with all of the Windows CE remnant code and created this operating system completely from scratch.

**The Windows Phone 7 operating
system looks a lot different from
Windows Mobile.**

It is worth noting that the original Windows Phone 7 release lacked many of the features that I write about in this book. In late 2011, Microsoft released a major update to the operating system (Windows Phone 7.5) which added over 500 new features. However, many of the new features are geared toward developers and are not exposed to the end user. Even so, Windows Phone 7.5 is a tremendous improvement over the original Windows Phone 7 release.

Except in cases where the difference is specifically relevant to you, I do not, in this book, distinguish between Windows Phone version 7 and version 7.5. The text and screenshots used are entirely based on the 7.5 version of the operating system, which every Windows Phone 7 user has access to.

My Impressions of Windows Phone 7

I have to admit that the first time that I was exposed to the Windows Phone 7 operating system, I was a little put off. It seemed that Microsoft had completely dumbed down the interface in an effort to appeal to technophobes. The Windows desktop had been replaced by a series of tiles, and many of the features I had been accustomed to since my first experiences with Windows CE back in 1998 were simply gone.

Even though I was less than thrilled about the new operating system, I knew I needed to learn about all of its features and nuances. I make a living writing about all things Windows, and like it or not, this was a Windows phone.

As I learned more about the new operating system, my opinion of it slowly changed. Although I will be the first to admit that there are some Windows Mobile 6.x features that I really wish Microsoft had included in the Windows Phone 7 operating system, there was simply no denying that the phone could do things that my Windows Mobile 6.5 phone couldn't. I had to upgrade.

After a while, I was glad I decided to replace my Windows Mobile 6.5 phone with a Windows Phone 7 device. The new mobile version of Internet Explorer is a huge improvement over what was previously available, and the improvements in Microsoft Office Mobile finally made it possible for me to read my editors' comments when they send me questions about something I have written.

Of course that was just the first Windows Phone 7 release. Since that time, Microsoft has made a number of improvements to Windows Phone 7, including the much anticipated "Mango" update, which upgraded the phone to Windows Mobile 7.5.

Mango has proven to be a phenominal update that turned a good mobile operating system into a great one. As with any operating system, there are things I like and things I don't like about Windows Phone 7.5. Some of my favorite Windows Phone 7 features include

- Native support for multiple email accounts.

- Integrated Facebook support.

- The ability to play YouTube videos.

- A much, much better Web browser. Windows Phone 7 runs a version of Internet Explorer 9 that is similar to what you might find on a desktop PC.

- An improved version of Microsoft Office Mobile that now supports things like comments within documents and Excel charts.

- The operating system can be kept up to date through patches provided by Microsoft.

- The devices use a faster processor than previous Windows Mobile devices and are therefore more responsive.

- Windows Phone 7 devices seem to be quite durable. I wrote a good portion of this book while on an expedition to Antarctica. Before the trip, I really wasn't sure how well the phone would handle the cold. I expected the liquid in the LCD screen to freeze and for the battery to lose its charge. However, the device performed very well, even when I ventured outside to try out the device's camera.

This photo was taken with a Windows Phone 7 device while on an expedition to Antarctica.

As I mentioned before, Windows Phone 7 does have some shortcomings. Some of the things I don't like about Windows Phone 7 include the following:

- It is no longer possible to access the device's file system, and you can't mount the device as a USB storage device.

- Unlike Windows Mobile 6.x, there is no option to enroll the device in a Windows domain.

- Microsoft has done away with the screen capture API. If some of the images in this book look a little fuzzy it's because I had to photograph the device screen rather than taking a screen capture.

- You can only install apps from the Marketplace. If you want to install homebrew code, you have to pay for a developer account and then unlock your phone.

- Microsoft introduced some new security features in Windows Phone 7.5. This caused some apps that were developed for the original Windows Phone 7 release to break.

Even with these negatives, Windows Phone 7 is a compelling competitor to Android smartphones and the iPhone. You'll see why as I take you through all of the phone's ins and outs throughout the rest of this book.

Soon you will be wondering how you ever got along without your Windows Phone 7 device!

In this chapter, you learn the basics of working with Windows Phone 7. First, you learn about all of the device's physical features. After that, you learn how to prepare the phone for its first use and how to install the Zune software. Finally, you learn the basics of interacting with your phone.

1

Getting Started with Windows Phone 7

Minimum Hardware Specifications

Microsoft requires all Windows Phone manufacturers to adhere to certain minimum hardware specifications. As a result, all Windows Phone 7 devices contain the following minimum hardware:

- A Qualcomm Snapdragon processor

- DirectX graphics hardware support with hardware acceleration for Direct3D using programmable GPU

- A minimum of 256MB of RAM

- A minimum of 8GB flash memory

- 802.11 b/g wireless (802.11n is optional)

- Bluetooth

- FM Radio

- A four-point multitouch capacitive touch screen

- GPS

- An accelerometer

- A magnetometer (compass)

- A proximity sensor

- A light sensor

- 800x480 WVGA display resolution with minimum 16 bits of color per pixel

- A minimum 5-megapixel camera

- A minimum of VGA resolution video capture

- Start, Back, and Search buttons

- Power, Volume Up, and Volume Down buttons

- Two-stage Camera button

- Vibration motor

- Micro-USB 2.0

- 3.5mm stereo headset jack with three-button detection support

---

Not All Phones Are Created Equal

The hardware specifications listed here represent the minimum hardware required by Microsoft. However, some phone manufacturers equip Windows Phone 7 devices with additional hardware. For example, some of the phones that are currently on the market include additional storage, a hardware keyboard, or surround sound speakers.

The Phone's External Features

Although Windows Phone 7 is designed to be used primarily through the touch screen interface, the phone does include a few hardware buttons that are designed to make the phone easier to use.

A. **The Power button**—The Power button turns the phone or the phone's display on and off.

B. **The Start button**—Pressing the Start button takes you to the phone's Start screen. It can also be used to access the phone's speech recognition functions.

C. **The Back button**—Pressing the Back button takes you to the previous screen or to the Task Switcher.

D. **The Search button**—The Search button takes you to an interface that helps you to locate information quickly.

E. **The Volume buttons**—The Volume buttons allow you to adjust the device's volume.

F. **The Camera button**—Pressing the Camera button activates the device's camera. After that the button can be pressed half way to focus the camera or all the way to snap a photo.

In addition to the phone's hardware buttons, there are a few other external features you need to know about.

A.   USB port—The USB port is used for charging the device and for connecting the device to a PC.

B.   Headphone jack—The headphone jack is used for listening to media through headphones or for hands free phone conversations.

C.   Camera lens—Windows Phone 7 includes a camera that can be used to take still photos and videos.

D.   Optical sensor—The optical sensor is used to automatically adjust the brightness of the display.

E.   Battery cover—The battery and the SIM card are found beneath the battery cover.

F.   Hardware keyboard—Some Windows Phone 7 models include an optional hardware keyboard that slides from beneath the screen.

(F)

The Initial Configuration

When you power up your Windows phone for the first time, you will have to work through a short configuration wizard before the phone is ready to use. The phone gives you the choice of performing a setup with the recommended settings or with custom settings. The recommended settings are almost always acceptable, but both configurations are presented here.

Configuring the Phone Using the Recommended Settings

To configure the phone using the recommended settings, follow these steps:

1. Turn on the phone.

2. Tap Get Started

3. Choose your language.

4. Tap Next.

5. Tap Accept to accept the license agreement.

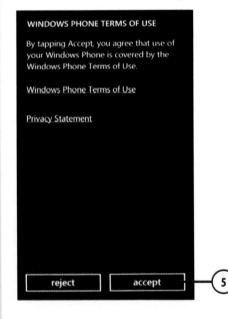

6. Tap Recommended to set the phone up using the recommended settings.

7. Choose your time zone.

8. Tap Next.

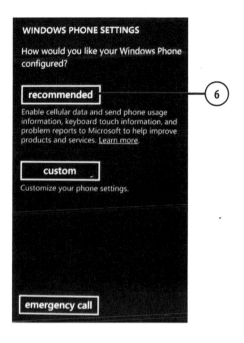

9. Enter the correct date and time.

10. Tap Next.

11. When prompted to sign in with a Windows Live ID, tap Not Now. Windows Live is discussed in a later chapter.

12. Tap Done.

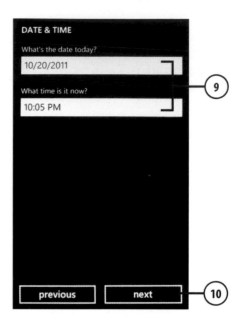

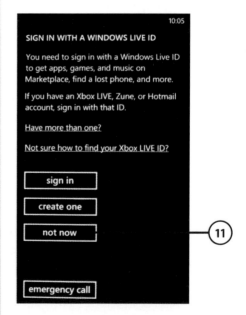

Configuring the Phone Using Custom Settings

Performing a custom setup is similar to performing a recommended setup except that you are given the option of whether or not you want to allow the use of cellular data. You are also given the chance to provide Microsoft with usage data that will help to improve the Windows Phone operating system. To perform a custom setup, complete these steps.

1. Tap Get Started
2. Choose your language.
3. Tap Next.
4. Tap Accept to accept the license agreement.

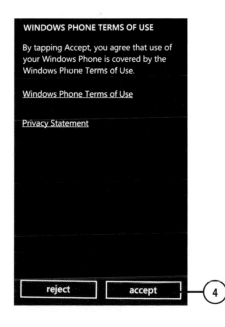

5. Tap Custom to set the phone up using custom settings.

6. Select the Allow Cellular Data Usage on Your Phone check box.

7. Decide whether or not you want to select the Send Information to Help Improve Windows Phones check box.

8. Tap Next.

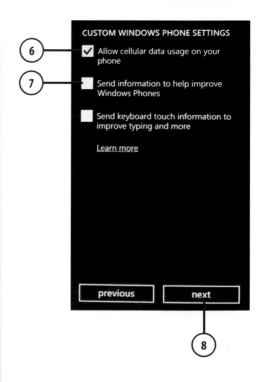

9. Choose your time zone.

10. Tap Next.

11. Enter the correct date and time.

12. Tap Next.

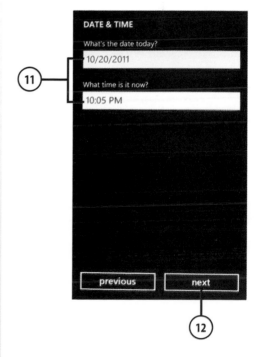

13. When prompted to sign in with a Windows Live ID, tap Not Now. Windows Live is discussed in a later chapter.

14. Tap Done.

Avoiding Excessive Phone Bills

If you have a cellular plan that charges you based on the amount of data that you use, then you should perform a custom setup and deselect the option to send information to help improve Windows phones. This will help to reduce your phone bills.

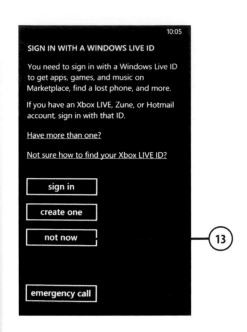

Install the Zune Software

Microsoft's Zune software is used to import media files into Windows Phone and to apply firmware updates to the phone. As such, the Zune software should be considered essential for all Windows Phone users.

Installing Zune Software

1. Download the Zune software from http://www.zune.com.

2. When prompted, click Run to run the Zune Setup Package (SuneSetupPkg.exe).

3. Click Run again to run the Zune software.

4. Accept the license agreement.

5. Click Install.

6. When Setup completes, click Close. It might be necessary to reboot your computer.

4

5

6

Adding the Phone to Zune

The first time you plug your phone
into your computer via the USB
cable, you will have to perform a few
steps that will allow Windows to
identify your phone:

1. When Windows displays the Zune
   Start screen, click Next.

2. When prompted, provide the software with a name for your phone.
   The phone's make and model is
   used as the default name.

3. Click Next.

4. Allow the Zune software to check
   for updates.

5. When prompted, provide Zune with the names of three of your favorite artists. The phone's entertainment capabilities are covered in a later chapter, but specifying your favorite artists is part of the initial Zune setup.

6. Click Done.

Updating the Phone

Like desktop and server versions of Windows, Microsoft occasionally releases updates to the Windows Phone 7 operating system. These updates might correct bugs, enhance security, or add new features. You can check for updates by using either the Zune software or the phone itself.

Using the Zune Software to Check for Updates

To check for available updates using the Zune software:

1. Attach your phone to your PC via a USB cable.

2. Open the Zune software.

3. Click Settings.

4. When the Settings screen appears, choose the Phone option.

5. Click Update.

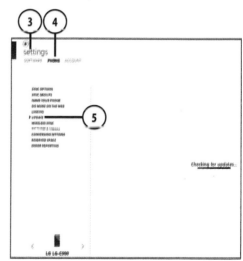

Checking for Updates Without the Zune Software

You can configure your phone to automatically check for available updates regardless of whether or not you use the Zune software by taking the following steps:

1. Tap the Start button.

2. Flick the arrow icon to access the App List.

3. Scroll to the bottom of the App List and tap Settings.

4. Tap Phone Update.

5. Select the Notify Me When New Updates are Found check box.

6. You can optionally select the Use My Cellular Data Connection to Check for Updates check box.

DOWNLOADING UPDATES

Go Further

It is generally recommended that you do not use the cellular connection to check for updates. Some updates can be quite large, and you can consume a lot of air time and battery power if you download such updates over a cellular connection. Updates can be downloaded much more quickly using a Wi-Fi connection.

The New Interface

The Windows Phone operating system was designed completely from scratch, and as such the user interface is nothing like Microsoft has ever created before. The new interface is designed so that you can interact with virtually all aspects of the operating system using a touch screen.

The Lock Screen

When you turn on a Windows Phone device, the first thing you see is the Lock screen. Although this screen initially looks like nothing more than a wallpaper screen, it provides several pieces of information.

A. **Cellular signal strength**—This indicator displays the signal strength as a series of bars. It also shows you when no cellular service is available.

B. **Wireless Connection type**—This is an icon that displays the type of wireless connection. For example, the icon could indicate 3G connectivity.

C. **Wi-Fi indicator**—This icon shows you whether or not Wi-Fi is enabled.

D. **Bluetooth indicator**—This is an icon which indicates whether or not Bluetooth is enabled.

E. **Battery Strength**—The battery indicator shows how much battery power remains.

F. **Time**—The current time.

G. **Date**—Today's date.

H. **Message indicator**—The bottom of the lock screen might contain icons indicating you have missed calls or that you have new email or text messages.

Clearing the Lock Screen

You can get past the Lock screen by touching the wallpaper and flicking it upward.

The Start Screen

The Start screen (which can be accessed by pressing the Start button) contains a series of tiles, which Microsoft refers to as *live tiles*. Live tiles serve two different purposes. First, you can access commonly used portions of the operating system by tapping the appropriate live tile. Second, live tiles are often dynamically updated to provide important information through the tile itself. For instance live tiles can tell you how many email messages you have waiting or how many calls you have missed. These are the tiles present on the Start screen by default:

A. **Phone**—The Phone tile provides one-touch access to the dialing pad. The tile also displays the current number of missed calls.

B. **People**—The People tile provides access to your contact list (known as the People Hub). The tile displays thumbnails of the profile photos used within your contacts.

C. **Messaging**—The Messaging tile displays the number of unread SMS text messages. You can tap the tile to access the messaging app.

D. **Outlook**—The Outlook tile displays the total number of unread email messages while also providing one-touch access to Outlook.

E. **Internet Explorer**—The Internet Explorer tile provides access to Internet Explorer.

F. **XBOX Live**—The XBOX Live tile provides access to your collection of games.

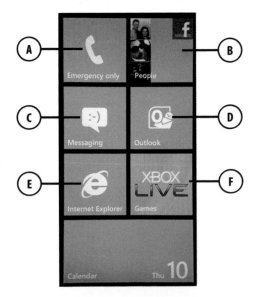

Too Many Default Tiles

The Start screen contains too many default tiles to display them all at once. You can access additional default tiles by flicking the Start screen upward.

G. Calendar—The Calendar tile displays your next appointment and provides one-touch access to the device's calendar.

H. Pictures—The Pictures tile provides access to your photo collection. The tile itself displays one of your photos.

I. Music + Video—This tile provides access to multimedia content that is stored on the phone.

J. Marketplace—The Marketplace is Microsoft's app store. This tile can sometimes display a numerical value indicating the number of updates available for the apps you have purchased.

K. Me—The Me tile dynamically displays your profile picture and links you to information about you that was downloaded from social networking sites.

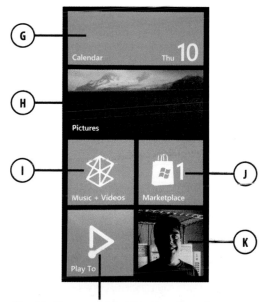

The Play To tile was added by the phone's manufacturer and is not a part of the Windows Phone 7.5 operating system.

Extra Tiles

Some phone manufacturers include extra tiles on the Start screen. For example, AT&T includes a tile for AT&T U-verse Mobile. Any extra tiles that might be present on the Start screen by default are manufacturer-specific and are not a part of the core Windows Phone 7 operating system.

Using the Phone's Hardware Buttons

As you saw at the beginning of the chapter, the front of the phone contains three hardware buttons. These buttons perform a variety of functions depending on whether they are pressed or held.

The Back Button

Pressing the Back button returns you to the previous screen. In some cases this can be a bit disorientating, however, because if your previous screen was the Start screen, the phone will usually skip it and take you instead to the screen that you were viewing prior to the Start screen.

If you hold down the Back button, Windows displays the Task Switcher, which is new to Windows Phone 7. The Task Switcher displays a series of recently visited screens so you can pick the screen you want to return to without having to repeatedly press the Back button.

The Start Button

Pressing the Start button from anywhere in the operating system will take you to the phone's Start screen. Holding down on the Start button takes you to the Voice Command screen. Voice control is covered in detail in Chapter 9, "Search," along with verbal searches.

Pressing and holding the Start button reveals the phone's voice recognition interface.

The Search Button

Pressing the Search button takes you to a search engine. The exact type of search that is provided varies depending on what screen you were viewing when you pressed the Search button. Searches are discussed at length in Chapter 9.

The Power Button

Pressing the Power button turns off the phone's display. You can turn the display back on by pressing the Power button again. When you turn off the display, the phone is still active. It can still receive phone calls, text messages, and so on.

If you need to completely shut down the phone, you can do so by pressing and holding the Power button. After several seconds, the phone displays a Zune style Shut-down screen that requires you to swipe the screen downward in order to shut down the phone. You can power the phone back up by pressing the Power button.

Press and hold the Power button and then flick the screen downward to shut down the phone.

Touch Gestures

Windows Phone uses a multi-touch display that supports six distinct touch gestures. These gestures include

- **Tap**—In the Windows Phone OS, a tap works exactly like it did in previous versions of Windows Mobile. You simply tap your finger on an object to select it.

- **Double-tap**—Windows Phone allows you to open files and applications by double-tapping them.

- **Pan**—Panning allows you to scroll the device's screen. You simply press your finger onto the device screen and then move your finger in the direction that you want to pan. The main Windows Phone screen contains too many tiles to fit all of them onto the screen at once, so you must pan the screen to access some of the tiles.

- **Flick**—Flicking allows you to scroll rapidly through a long list of items. Flicking is similar to panning except that once you have pressed your finger onto the screen, you slide it quickly and then remove your finger.

- **Touch and Hold**—The touch and hold gesture is used similarly to right-clicking your mouse in Windows 7. You simply press an object on the screen and then hold your finger in the same position until any available options are displayed. For example, you can use the touch and hold gesture to pin an item to the Start screen.

- **Stretch**—Stretching is a gesture that you can use to make an object on the screen bigger. For example, you might use the stretch gesture to zoom in on a picture, or you could use the stretch gesture to zoom in on an area within your Web browser. You can stretch an area by placing two fingers onto the screen and then sliding those fingers apart.

- **Pinch**—Pinching is the opposite of stretching. It is used as a way to zoom out. To pinch, spread two fingers apart and then put them on the screen and slide your fingers until they come together.

The Soft Keyboard

The primary method of entering text into Windows Phone is through a soft (on screen) keyboard. Rather than providing you with a generic soft keyboard, Windows Phone uses one of seven different soft keyboards depending on the activity being performed. These soft keyboards include:

A. **Default**—A standard QWERTY keyboard layout.

A standard QWERTY keyboard

B. **Text**—A standard QWERTY layout, plus emoticons.

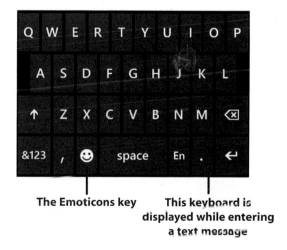

The Emoticons key   **This keyboard is displayed while entering a text message**

C. Email Address—QWERTY layout plus a .com and an @ key.

The @ key   The .COM Key

D. Phone Number—A twelve key phone layout.

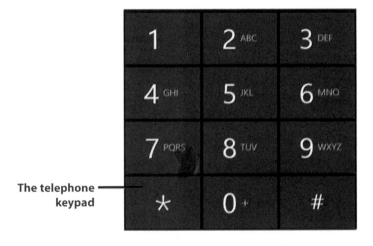

The telephone keypad

E. Web Address—QWERTY layout plus a .com key and a custom Enter key.

The .COM key

The custom Enter key

F.   Search and Maps—QWERTY layout plus a custom Enter key.

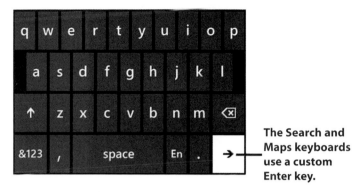

The Search and Maps keyboards use a custom Enter key.

G.   SMS Address—QWERTY layout with access to the phone layout.

When specifying the recipient of an SMS (text) message this key can be pressed to reveal the telephone keypad.

LOST KEYS

You might occasionally discover that the soft keyboard is missing some of the keys you need to use. When this happens, look for either a left or right arrow key. Tapping this key causes Windows to reveal additional keys on the soft keyboard. You can sometimes also access additional keys by tapping and holding keys. For example tapping and holding the period key causes other punctuation keys (comma, question mark, and so on) to be revealed.

Go Further

Typing with the soft keyboard can take a little bit of getting used to. The soft keyboard lacks the tactical feel of a hardware keyboard, and the screen's size limits the size of the keys. As such, typing can be a little bit tricky. Fortunately, there are a few things you can do to make typing easier.

One suggestion is to turn the phone sideways. When you do, the display changes to a landscape orientation. This causes the keys on the soft keyboard to become wider, which makes typing easier.

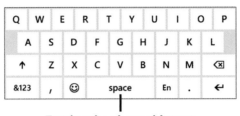

Turning the phone sideways makes the keyboard larger.

Windows Phone 7 suggests words as you type.

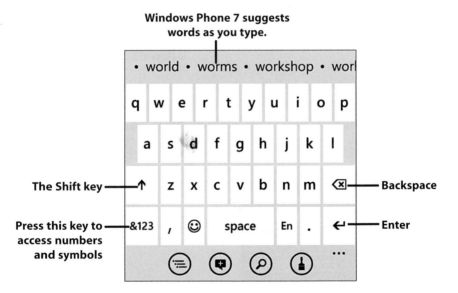

The Shift key ———

Backspace

Press this key to ——— &123
access numbers
and symbols

Enter

As you type, Windows suggests words based on the letters you have entered. You can tap on a suggested word rather than having to type the entire word.

The soft keyboard does not contain a caps lock key. To activate Caps Lock, simply tap and hold the shift key for a few seconds. Repeat the process to release Caps Lock.

Keyboard Configuration

Windows Phone allows you to configure the behavior of the keyboard, including whether or not suggestions are displayed as you type. The various keyboard configuration options are discussed in Chapter 2, "Basic Device Settings."

The Hardware Keyboard

Some Windows Phone devices include a hardware keyboard that slides out from beneath the screen. Hardware keyboards typically include a few specialized keys including

A. **Shift**—The Shift key is displayed as an up arrow and toggles between uppercase and lowercase text.

B. **Function**—The function key is usually displayed as FN and switches between letters and the number or symbols displayed in blue.

C. **AE**—Displays an onscreen keyboard containing foreign variations of the character that was most recently typed.

D. **Symbols**—On some phones the Symbol (SYM) key does the same thing as the function (FN) key.

E. **Emoticons**—Displays an onscreen keyboard containing a series of emoticons.

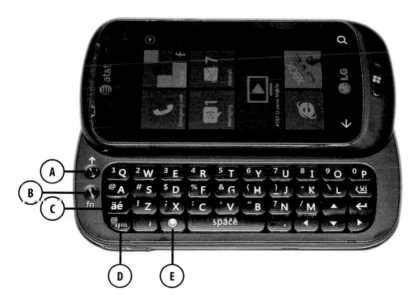

Customizing the Start Screen

Windows Phone does not require you to use the default tile layout. You are free to add, remove, and rearrange the tiles to meet your own individual preferences.

Moving a Tile

To rearrange the tiles on the Start screen

1. Tap and hold the tile you want to move.

2. When the tile's appearance changes, drag the tile to the desired location.

3. When the tile is in its new location, lift your finger and then tap the tile one last time.

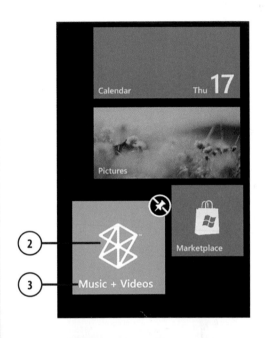

Removing a Tile

To Remove a tile from the Start screen:

1. Tap and hold the tile until its appearance changes.

2. Tap the unpin button that is displayed in the upper right-hand corner of the tile.

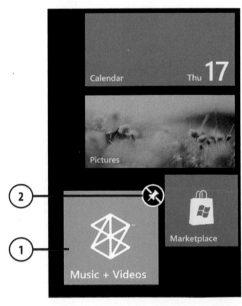

Adding a Tile

Virtually any object can be pinned to the Start screen. For example, you can pin an application to the Start screen, or you can pin an individual person from your contacts to the Start screen. That way, you can access that person's contact information and social networking updates with a single touch. To pin an object to the Start screen

1. Press and hold the object.

2. When the object's menu appears, tap the Pin to Start option.

3. The object is added to the bottom of the Start screen but can be moved to any position.

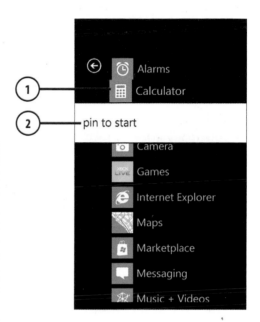

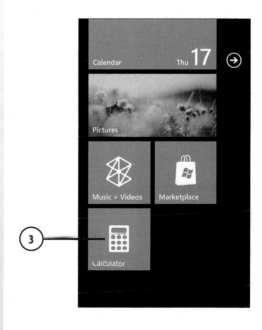

Resetting Your Phone

It is possible to reset your phone to its factory settings should the need ever arise. Please keep in mind that resetting your phone causes all data and apps to be erased from the phone. If you have downloaded and installed apps directly to the phone, those apps will be gone for good. However, apps that are downloaded and installed through the Zune software can be reinstalled without having to repurchase them. Apps that were built into the phone by the manufacturer will be automatically reinstalled when the phone is reset. To reset your phone, follow these steps:

1. Press the Start button.

2. Flick the arrow icon to the left to access the App List (which is covered in the next chapter).

3. Scroll to the bottom of the App List and tap Settings.

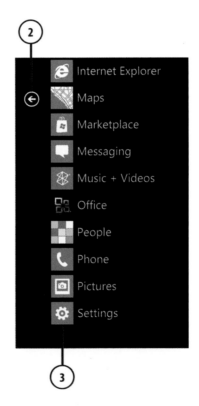

4. Tap About.

5. Scroll to the bottom of the screen.

6. Tap Reset Your Phone.

7. Read the warning message and then tap Yes.

8. When Windows asks you if you are sure, tap Yes.

9. The phone is automatically powered off as a part of the reset process.

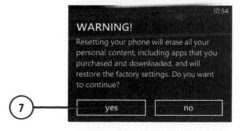

The System Settings page provides access to many of the device's configuration options.

In the previous chapter you learned that it is possible to customize Windows Phone's Start screen. However, there are many other ways in which you can personalize your phone. In this chapter, you learn how to apply themes to your phone and how to perform a wide variety of other personalizations. In addition, this chapter also walks you through the various available settings.

2

Basic Device Settings

Accessing the Device Settings

Most of the procedures outlined in this chapter involve using the phone's Settings screen. You can access the Settings screen by doing the following:

1. Press the Start button.

2. Flick the arrow icon to the left to access the App list.

3. Scroll through the App list until you locate the Settings option.

4. Tap Settings.

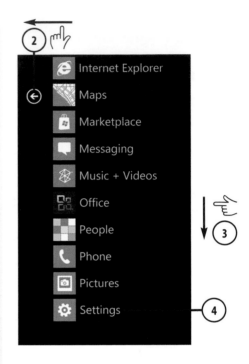

The Settings page contains most of the phone's settings.

Settings are divided among a System Settings and an Applications Settings page.

Themes

1. Press the Start button.

2. Flick the arrow icon to go to the App list.

3. Tap Settings.

4. Tap Theme.

5. Set the background to either Dark or Light.

6. Choose an Accent color.

SETTINGS

theme

Change your phone's background and
accent color to match your mood today,
this week, or all month.

Background

dark ————————— ⑤

Accent color

■ red ————————— ⑥

Wi-Fi Networking

Even though Windows Phone is designed to access the Internet through a
cellular connection, the phone also supports Wi-Fi connectivity. Wi-Fi connections allow for faster Internet connectivity than what is possible through a
cellular link, and using Wi-Fi has the added benefit of not incurring any data
charges on your cellular bill. All Windows Phone 7 devices include support for
802.11B and 802.11G with some phones also offering 802.11N support.

Enabling or Disabling Wi-Fi

You can enable or disable Wi-Fi on a Windows Phone device by following these steps:

1. Press the Start button.

2. Flick the arrow icon to access the App List.

3. Tap Settings.

4. Tap Wi-Fi.

5. Use the Slidebar to enable or Disable Wi-Fi.

Connecting to a Wi-Fi Network

To connect a Windows Phone 7 device to a Wi-Fi network, follow these steps:

1. Press the Start button.

2. Flick the arrow icon to access the App List.

3. Tap Settings.

4. Tap Wi-Fi.

5. Verify that Wi-Fi Networking is enabled.

6. Select the Notify Me When New Networks are Found check box is selected.

7. Tap the Wi-Fi network you want to connect to.

8. If prompted, enter the network password. If you have trouble entering the password blindly, you can select the Show Password check box to make the password visible.

9. Tap Done.

10. Next you see a message indicating you are connected to the wireless network.

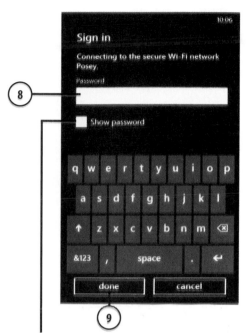

If you are having trouble entering the password correctly, you can make the process easier by using this check box to make the password visible.

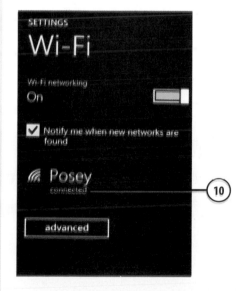

It's Not All Good

Some of the first Windows Phone 7 devices made available contain a bug, which causes Wi-Fi passwords to be accepted only on an intermittent basis. Even if you enter a password correctly, you might receive an incorrect password error. If you successfully establish a Wi-Fi connection, the password (which is stored in the device with the connection) might not be accepted the next time you use the device. This bug is also known to cause Wi-Fi connections to drop without warning.

The Wi-Fi bug was supposed to have been corrected shortly after the devices were made publically available, but some of the older phones still have Wi-Fi problems, even after being upgraded to Windows Phone 7.5. Thankfully the newer Windows phones do not seem to have this problem.

When a phone simply refuses to connect to Wi-Fi, it is sometimes possible to force the connection by turning off Wi-Fi support, resetting the wireless access point, and then turning Wi-Fi support back on.

Support for Hidden Wireless Networks

The original Windows Phone 7 release was only capable of connecting to wireless networks that broadcast their SSID (the wireless network's identification). However, some organizations disable SSID broadcasts to hide their wireless networks. Windows Phone 7.5 fully supports connecting to hidden Wi-Fi networks.

Removing Known Networks

Windows Phone is designed to remember the settings for every Wi-Fi network you connect to. If you tend to connect your phone to public Wi-Fi hotspots, you will eventually accumulate a long list of known networks. Some of these networks might be Wi-Fi hotspots you will never connect to again. Fortunately, Windows Phone provides an easy way to delete references to unwanted wireless networks. To remove these networks

1. Press the Start button.

2. Flick the arrow icon to access the App List.

3. Tap Settings.

4. Tap Wi-Fi.

5. Tap Advanced.

6. Tap the Select icon.

7. Select the check boxes for each network that you want to remove.

8. Tap the Delete icon.

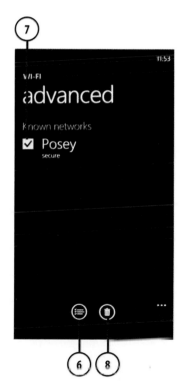

Changing Wallpaper

Just as you can configure desktop versions of Windows to display a personalized wallpaper image, so too can you change the wallpaper that is used by Windows Phone. To do so, perform the following steps:

1. Press the Start button.

2. Flick the arrow icon to go to the App list.

3. Tap Settings.

4. Tap Lock + Wallpaper.

5. Tap Change Wallpaper.

6. Choose either Camera Roll, an album, or the Wallpapers container. The Camera Roll option allows you to choose a photo that you have taken with the built in camera. Similarly, picking an album allows you to choose a photo from that album. The Wallpapers option allows you to use the built-in wallpapers.

7. Tap the wallpaper of choice.

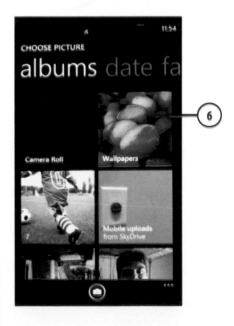

8. Tap the Crop icon to accept your choice or tap the Back button to go back to the wallpaper selection screen.

The wallpaper you choose is only displayed on the phone's Lock screen.

Screen Time Out

In an effort to preserve battery life and improve security, Windows Phone is designed to time out after a period of inactivity. When the timeout threshold is reached, the device's screen is automatically turned off. You can adjust the timeout threshold period by following these steps:

1. Press the Start button.

2. Flick the arrow icon to go to the App list.

3. Tap Settings.

4. Tap Lock + Wallpaper.

5. Choose the screen timeout period. You can choose 30 seconds, 1 minute, 3 minutes, 5 minutes, or never.

Saving Changes

The Lock + Wallpaper screen does not have any kind of button that you can press to make Windows accept the changes that you have made. If you change the screen timeout period, your change goes into effect as soon as you select a new timeout period.

Passwords

Few electronic devices contain as much sensitive information as a smart phone. If someone were to steal your cell phone they could potentially use the information stored in your phone to determine:

- Where you live

- When you will be away from home (by looking at the information in your calendar)

- The names and contact information of your friends, family, and business associates

As if that were not enough, someone who is in possession of your phone could send email messages posing as you, or they could run up your phone bill by placing a bunch of international calls. As such, you need to protect your Windows Phone device just as you would protect a laptop that was loaded with personal information.

Enable a Password

The single most important thing you can do to protect your phone is to configure it to require a password for access. To enable the password requirement, complete the following steps:

1. Press the Start button.

2. Flick the arrow icon to go to the App list.

3. Tap Settings.

4. Tap Lock + Wallpaper.

5. Set the Password slidebar to On.

6. When prompted, enter a numeric password.

7. Tap Confirm Password.

8. Re-enter your password.

9. Tap Done.

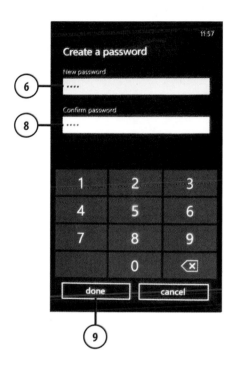

Don't Forget Your Password

If you use a password with your Windows Phone device, be careful not to forget it. There is no way to retrieve a lost password. If you forget your password you will be forced to reset the device to its factory defaults, which means losing your data and your apps.

Change Your Password

Most security professionals agree that it is a good idea to change your password on a regular basis. You can change your password by completing these steps:

1. Press the Start button.

2. Flick the arrow icon to go to the App list.

3. Tap Settings.

4. Tap Lock + Wallpaper.

5. Tap Change Password.

6. Enter your previous password.

7. Enter a new password.

8. Re-enter your new password.

9. Tap Done.

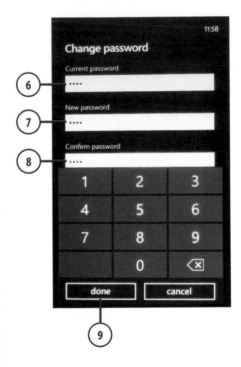

Disable a Password

Although not necessarily recommended, it is possible to disable your device's password so that you are no longer required to enter a password to access the device. To disable a password, complete these steps:

1. Tap Settings.

2. Tap Lock + Wallpaper

3. Set the Password slidebar to Off.

4. When prompted, enter your password.

Date and Time

Although it might seem trivial, it is important to ensure that the phone's date and time are set correctly. Some of the phone's functions do not work correctly unless the phone is set to use the correct date and time. For example, you receive an error message if the date and time on your phone is incorrect when you attempt to connect to Microsoft Live.

Windows Phone provides two methods for setting the date and time. You can set the date and time manually, or you can have the phone do it automatically.

Setting the Date and Time Automatically

Windows Phone's default behavior is to set the date and time automatically. If you want to verify this behavior or if you want to go back to using an automatic date and time setting after having manually set the date and time, you can do so by completing these steps:

1. Press the Start button.

2. Flick the arrow icon to access the App List.

3. Scroll to the bottom of the App List and tap Settings.

4. Tap Date + Time.

5. Set the Set Automatically slidebar to On.

Not Completely Automated

Even though this procedure does a good job of keeping the date and time set correctly, you are still required to manually set the date and time the first time you turn on the phone. If you skip that step and leave the time set to its default of 12:00, the time remains incorrect.

Setting the Date and Time Manually

If you prefer to set the date and time manually, you can easily accomplish this by following these steps:

1. Press the Start button.

2. Flick the arrow icon to access the App List.

3. Scroll to the bottom of the App List and tap Settings.

4. Tap Date and Time.

5. Set the Set Automatically slidebar to Off.

6. Tap Time.

7. Set the time.

8. Tap the Done icon when you are done.

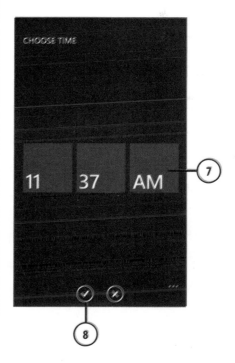

9. Tap Date.

10. Set the date.

11. Tap the Done icon when you are done.

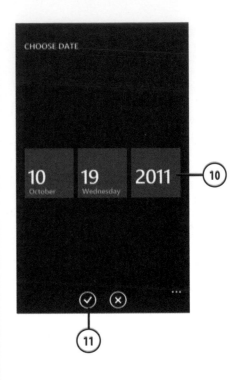

Changing Time Zones

If you travel with your phone, you might need to set the phone to a different time zone as you move from place to place. Changing the phone's time zone causes the clock to change to reflect the local time in your current location. However, if you can receive a cell signal, then the phone usually changes time zones automatically without you having to do anything. If you do need to manually switch time zones, you can do so by completing these steps:

1. Press the Start button.

2. Flick the arrow icon to access the App List.

3. Scroll to the bottom of the App List and tap Settings.

4. Tap Date and Time.

5. Set the Set Automatically slidebar to Off.

6. Tap Time Zone.

7.   Choose your desired time zone.

Time Zones and Your Calendar

When you change time zones—whether manually or automatically—any appointments stored in your calendar will shift to reflect the local time. For example, if you start out in the Eastern time zone and enter a 2:30 appointment and then fly out to the west coast, the calendar displays the appointment as occurring at 11:30 in response to the time zone change.

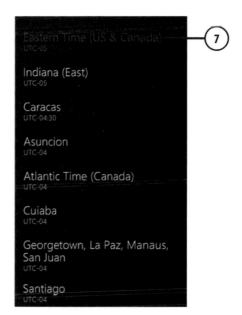

Eastern Time (US & Canada)
UTC-05

Indiana (East)
UTC-05

Caracas
UTC-04:30

Asuncion
UTC-04

Atlantic Time (Canada)
UTC-04

Cuiaba
UTC-04

Georgetown, La Paz, Manaus, San Juan
UTC-04

Santiago
UTC-04

Using Military Time

Those who have served in the Armed Forces or who operate on a 24-hour clock might prefer to configure the phone to use military time. To enable military time, complete these steps:

1.   Press the Start button.

2.   Flick the arrow icon to access the App List.

3.   Scroll to the bottom of the App List and Tap Settings.

4.   Tap Date and Time.

5.   Slide the 24-Hour Clock slidebar to On.

SETTINGS

date+time

24-hour clock
On

Set automatically
Off

Time zone
UTC-05 Eastern Time (US & Canada)

Date
10/19/2011

Time
11:39

Disabling Military Time

If you need to revert from using military time to using standard time, you can do so by performing these steps:

1. Press the Start button.

2. Flick the arrow icon to access the App List.

3. Scroll to the bottom of the App List and tap Settings.

4. Tap Date and Time.

5. Slide the 24-Hour Clock slidebar to Off.

Screen Brightness

Windows Phone allows you to adjust the brightness of the screen either automatically (in response to the current lighting conditions) or manually to a level of your choosing.

Automatically Adjusting the Screen Brightness

Windows Phone can automatically adjust the screen's brightness based on the current lighting conditions. If you want the phone to adjust the screen's brightness automatically, perform these steps:

1. Press the Start button.

2. Flick the arrow icon to access the App List.

3. Scroll to the bottom of the App List and tap Settings.

4. Tap Brightness.

5. Set the Automatically Adjust slidebar to On.

Manually Adjusting the Screen Brightness

Manually adjusting the screen's brightness allows you to maintain a certain level of brightness regardless of the current lighting conditions. For example, Windows Phone is designed to automatically dim the screen when you are using the phone in a dark area and to brighten the screen when you are in a bright area. If you prefer to use your own brightness settings, then complete these steps to manually adjust the display's brightness:

1. Press the Start button.

2. Flick the arrow icon to access the App List.

3. Scroll to the bottom of the App List and tap Settings.

4. Tap Brightness.

5. Set the Automatically Adjust slidebar to Off.

6. Tap Level and choose your desired brightness level.

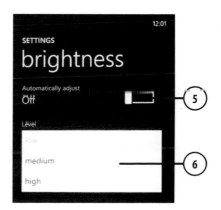

Controlling the Keyboard's Behavior

In Chapter 1, "Getting Started with Windows Phone 7," you saw how Windows Phone automatically suggests words as you type. However, you can control this and other behaviors through the phone's keyboard configuration settings.

Setting the Keyboard Language

Microsoft provides a number of different language selections for the Windows Phone keyboard. The language you choose affects the appearance of the soft keyboard as well as the words that are suggested as you type. You can configure the keyboard language by completing these steps:

1. Press the Start button.

2. Flick the arrow icon to access the App List.

3. Scroll to the bottom of the App List and tap Settings.

4. Tap Keyboard.

5. To set the keyboard language, tap Keyboard Languages and then choose your preferred language.

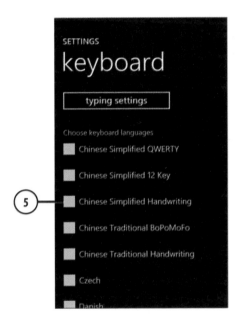

Clearing Custom Suggestions

As you compose e-mail and text messages you will occasionally use words that are not built into the phone's dictionary. Windows Phone pays attention to the words you use frequently and adds those words to the list of suggestions that are displayed as you type. The down side to this behavior is that if you frequently misspell words, then your phone might begin to suggest those misspellings. As such, Microsoft gives you a way to clear the phone's cache of custom suggestions. To clear the custom suggestion list, follow these steps:

1. Press the Start button.

2. Flick the arrow icon to reveal the App List.

3. Scroll to the bottom of the App List and tap Settings.

4. Tap Keyboard.

5. Tap Typing Settings.

6. Tap the Reset Suggestions button.

7. When prompted, tap the Reset button.

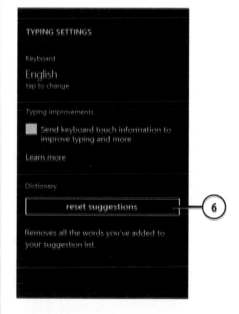

TYPING SETTINGS

Keyboard
English
tap to change

Typing improvements

☐ Send keyboard touch information to improve typing and more

Learn more

Dictionary

reset suggestions ⑥

Removes all the words you've added to your suggestion list.

It's Not All Good

In my opinion, this is one area of the operating system that Microsoft should have left alone. When you type words in Windows Phone 7.5, the operating system displays suggestions, but it also automatically corrects spelling and punctuation errors. Unfortunately, the auto correct function can be a nuisance if you are typing words that are not in the dictionary. The original Windows Phone 7 release contained an option to disable the automatic correction features, but this option has been removed from Windows Phone 7.5.

Region and Languages

The Region and Language settings allow you to configure localization information for the device. You can access the Region and Language settings by taking the following actions:

1. Press the Start button.

2. Flick the arrow icon to go to the App list.

3. Tap Settings.

4. Tap Region + Language.

The Region + Language screen contains several different settings, including

A. **Display Language**—The primary language that should be used on the device.

B. **Region Format**—The Region Format controls the way various region-specific parameters are displayed (such as currency).

C. **Short Date**—The format used when the date is displayed in a numerical format.

D. **Long Date**—The format that will be used when the date is displayed in its elongated form.

E. **First Day of the Week**—The day of the week you want to appear on the calendar as the first day of the week.

F. **System Locale**—The location in which you will be using the device.

G. **Browser and Search Language**—The language you want to use for Internet Explorer Mobile and Bing.

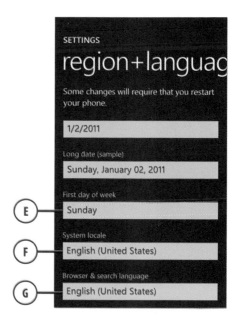

Accessibility

The Ease of Access settings allow you to enable or disable TTY and TTD mode (which are provided for the hearing impaired). You can access the Ease of Access settings by following these steps:

1. Press the Start button.

2. Flick the arrow icon to access the App List.

3. Scroll to the bottom of the list and tap Settings.

4. Tap Ease of Access.

The Ease of Access screen allows you to choose one of four different settings:

A. **Off**—Disable TTY and TTD Support.

B. **Full**—Full support for TTY and TTD.

C. **HCO (Hearing Carry Over)**— Enable Hearing Carry Over mode.

D. **VCO (Voice Carry Over)**—Enable Voice Carry Over mode.

Speech for Phone Accessibility
There is also a Speech for Phone Accessibility setting that can be used to enable verbal caller ID. This feature is discussed in Chapter 8, "The Phone."

Find My Phone

If your Windows Phone device is ever lost or stolen, you can use the Find My Phone feature to locate it. This feature allows you to locate your phone by forcing it to ring (even if it is on Silent or Vibrate mode) or by displaying the phone's location on a map. You also have the option of locking the phone or erasing its contents.

Prerequisite Requirement
To use the Find My Phone feature, your phone must be linked to a Windows Live account.

Configuring the Find My Phone Settings

Although anyone with cellular service can use the Find My Phone feature, it is a good idea to review your phone's configuration. Options exist that can help to improve your phone's location accuracy should you ever need to track down your phone. You can access these configuration options by performing these steps:

1. Press the Start button.

2. Flick the arrow icon to access the App List.

3. Scroll to the bottom of the list and tap Settings.

4. Tap Find My Phone.

The Find My Phone Screen offers you two different configuration options:

A. **Connect to These Features Faster**—Enabling this option helps to improve the accuracy of Find My Phone but also consumes more battery power.

B. **Save My Location Every Few Hours For Better Mapping**— This feature causes the phone to periodically save the phone's location.

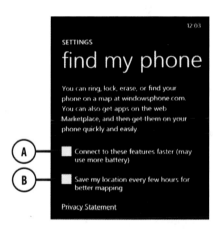

The Accuracy Tradeoff

Although enabling the two options just mentioned will help to improve the accuracy of the phone's locational awareness, it is worth noting that using these features can impact the phone's battery life. Furthermore, you should only use these options if you have an unlimited data plan because they cause the phone to transmit data that would not otherwise be sent.

Finding Your Phone

You have a few different options for finding your phone. You can cause the phone to ring, or you can display its location on a map. You also have the option of locking your phone or remotely erasing its contents. To access these features

1. From your computer, log into http://www.windowsphone.live. com by using your Windows Live account.

2. Click the Find This Phone link.

3. Click one of the following links:

   • **Map it**—Displays your phone's approximate location on a map.

   • **Ring It**—Force the phone to ring nonstop for one minute, even if the phone is on Silent or Vibrate.

   • **Lock It**—Use this option to lock your phone. You can even use this option to put a Please Return message on the phone's lock screen.

   • **Erase It**—Reset the phone to its factory settings.

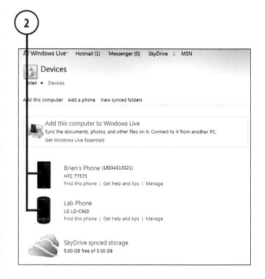

About Your Phone

The About option is designed primarily for those who need technical assistance. The About screen provides you with virtually everything you need when seeking help, including detailed information about the phone's hardware and firmware and contact information for the technical support department. The About screen also provides links to the phone's Terms of Use policy and privacy policy. You can access the About screen by following these steps:

1. Press the Start button.

2. Flick the arrow icon to access the App List.

3. Scroll to the bottom of the screen and tap Settings.

4. Tap About.

Phone version number

More Information button

Help contacts   **Online content terms of use**

Go Further

TECHNICAL SUPPORT REQUIREMENTS

If you ever have to call technical support about a problem with your phone, you might find that the support technician needs more detailed information about your phone's hardware and firmware versions than what is displayed on the About screen. If this ever happens to you, you can go to the About screen and tap the More Info button. Doing so causes the phone to reveal much more detailed version information.

Avoid Hitting the Reset Button!

The bottom of the About screen contains a button labeled Reset Your Phone (which was discussed in the previous chapter). Tapping this button causes your data and your apps to be permanently erased. Therefore, you should avoid tapping this button except as a last resort.

Providing Feedback

The Feedback option allows you to control whether or not user experience information is sent to Microsoft. The information that is collected is used to improve Windows Phone. If you do choose to enable the feedback feature, you have the option of controlling whether or not feedback information is sent using your cellular connection. To configure feedback

1. Press the Start button.

2. Flick the arrow icon to go to the App list.

3. Tap Settings.

4. Tap Feedback.

5. Use the slidebar to turn Feedback either on or off.

6. If Feedback is enabled, use the check box to control whether or not your cellular connection is used to send feedback data.

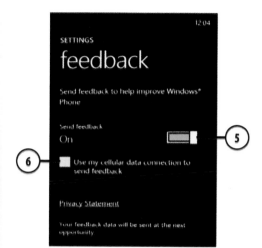

Protecting Your Privacy

Because your phone likely contains a lot of personal information, it is important to take steps to protect your privacy. As such, read Microsoft's privacy statement before enabling the Feedback feature. Furthermore, enabling this feature causes the phone to transmit extra data, so you should only enable the Feedback feature if you have an unlimited data plan.

In this chapter you will learn how to configure your Windows Phone 7 device to send and receive E-mail.

Messaging is one area in which Windows Phone really excels. Although many cell phones limit you to connecting to a single email account, Windows Phone 7 supports simultaneous connectivity to a virtually unlimited number of mailboxes. Furthermore, the phone offers native support for Microsoft Live, Exchange Server, Yahoo!, and Gmail. Of course, you also have the option of connecting to just about any mail server using POP3 or IMAP4.

Messaging

Setting Up a Windows Live Account

Regardless of whether or not you use Microsoft's Hotmail, you should set up a Windows Live account. Windows Live Accounts are used by Hotmail, XBOX Live, and Messenger. A Microsoft Live account is also required if you want to use the device's Find My Phone feature (which was discussed in Chapter 2, "Basic Device Settings"), Facebook Chat, or any number of other features. You can link the phone to your Microsoft Live account by completing these steps:

1. Press the Start button.

2. Flick the arrow icon to access the App List screen.

3. Scroll to the bottom of the App List screen and tap Settings.

4. Tap Email + Accounts.

5. Tap Add an Account.

6. Tap Windows Live.

7. Enter your email address and password.

8. Tap Sign In.

9. You are then returned to the Email + Account screen, and your Windows Live account is listed on the screen.

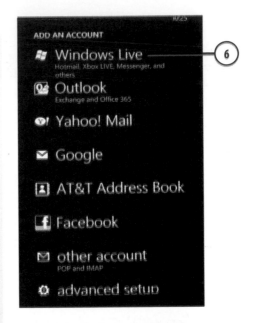

Setting Up Exchange Email

As you would probably expect, Windows Phone has the ability to connect to Exchange Server using ActiveSync. Microsoft provides two different methods for connecting to Exchange Server. The first method is a simplified method that only works with Exchange Server 2007 and 2010. The second method is a little more advanced and is used for connecting to older Exchange Servers or for attaching to Exchange Servers that do not fully support automatic configuration.

Simplified Exchange Server Connectivity

If you have an Exchange 2007 or 2010 server that supports automatic configuration for external clients, you can use the simplified connectivity method. To connect to your Exchange mailbox

1. Press the Start button.

2. Flick the arrow icon to access the App List screen.

3. Scroll to the bottom of the App List screen and tap Settings.

4. Tap Email + Account.

5. Tap Add an Account.

6. Tap Outlook.

7. Enter your email address and password.

8. Tap the Sign In button.

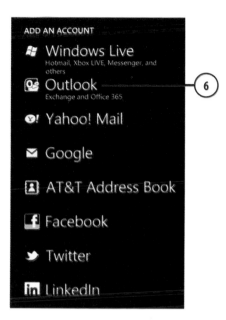

Advanced Exchange Server Connectivity

The connectivity method described in the previous section can only be used in ideal circumstances. Otherwise, you will have to use a more advanced method to establish Exchange Server connectivity. To do so, follow these steps:

1. Press the Start button.

2. Flick the arrow icon to go to the App List.

3. Scroll to the bottom of the App List and tap Settings.

4. Tap Email + Account.

5. Tap Add an Account.

6. Tap Advanced Setup.

7. Enter your Exchange email address and password.

8. Tap Next.

9. Tap Exchange ActiveSync.

10. Fill in the name of your Windows domain.

11. Enter the fully qualified domain name (FQDN) of your Client Access Server (or front end server for Exchange 2003 and earlier).

12. If your Exchange environment requires SSL encryption for ActiveSync, verify that the Server Requires Encrypted (SSL) Connection check box is selected. Otherwise deselect it.

ADVANCED SETUP

Choose the kind of account you want to set up. If you're not sure, check with your service provider.

Exchange ActiveSync ⑨
Includes Exchange and other accounts that use Exchange ActiveSync

Internet email
POP or IMAP accounts that let you view your email in a web browser

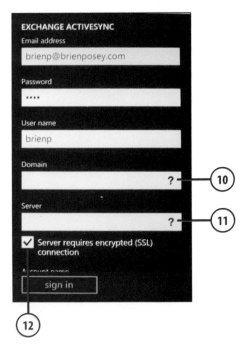

EXCHANGE ACTIVESYNC

Email address
brienp@brienposey.com

Password
••••

User name
brienp

Domain
? ⑩

Server
? ⑪

☑ Server requires encrypted (SSL) connection ⑫

Account name

sign in

13. Enter your name as you would like it to appear on outbound email messages into the Account Name field.

14. Set the Download New Content option to As Items Arrive.

15. Choose how much message history you would like to store on the phone (this will not affect your actual Exchange mailbox, only the amount of mail that is stored within the phone).

16. Choose the types of content you want to sync. Normally you will sync email, Contacts, and Calendar items.

17. Tap Sign In.

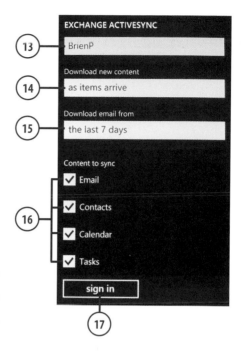

WHAT WENT WRONG?

You might discover that even after performing an advanced setup, Windows Phone is still unable to connect to Exchange Server. If this happens, verify you have spelled the fully qualified domain name of your Client Access Server correctly and that the server is externally accessible using this name. In some cases you might have to use the server's IP address rather than its name.

The other thing that tends to go wrong is that Windows Phone could have trouble using SSL encryption. The Exchange Server uses a certificate to perform SSL encryption. For Windows Phone to be able to use SSL encryption, the phone must trust the certificate authority that issued the certificate to Exchange. This is accomplished through the use of a CA certificate. Windows Phone has built-in CA certificates for the most popular commercial certificate authorities. However, if your company uses a certificate that was generated in-house or by a lesser known commercial certificate authority, the phone will not automatically trust the certificate authority, and SSL encryption will fail (which causes ActiveSync to fail).

The solution to this problem is to set up another mail account (such as a Windows Live Hotmail account or a Gmail account) and attach your phone to it. Next, ask your network administrator to email the required CA certificate to the account that you have just set up. When you receive the message, open the attachment, and the certificate will be installed on your phone. You should now be able to sync with Exchange Server.

One last problem that you may encounter is that mail may not synchronize even if everything is set up correctly. This can happen if you have told Windows Phone 7 to synchronize messages from the last 7 days, but all of the messages in your Inbox are more than 7 days old.

Connecting to Yahoo! Mail

Windows Phone includes native support for Yahoo! Mail. To link the phone to your Yahoo! account, complete these steps:

1. Tap the Start button.

2. Flick the arrow icon to access the App List.

3. Scroll to the bottom of the list and tap Settings.

4. Tap Email & Account.

5. Tap Add an Account.

6. Tap Yahoo! Mail.

7. Enter your Yahoo! email address and password.

8. Tap Sign In.

Connecting to Google Mail

Windows Phone offers native support for Google Mail (Gmail). To link the phone to your Gmail account, complete these steps:

1. Tap the Start button.

2. Flick the arrow icon to access the App List.

3. Scroll to the bottom of the list and tap Settings.

4. Tap Email + Account.

5. Tap Add an Account.

6. Tap Google.

7. Enter your Gmail email address and password.

8. Tap Sign In.

Setting Up POP3 / IMAP4 Messaging

If you need to connect Windows Phone to a mail system other than Windows Live, Exchange Server, Yahoo!, or Gmail, then you can do so by using a POP3/IMAP4 account. To establish connectivity to your mail server, perform the following steps:

1. Tap the Start button.

2. Flick the arrow icon to access the App List.

3. Scroll to the bottom of the list and tap Settings.

4. Tap Email + Account.

5. Tap Add an Account.

6. Tap Advanced Setup.

7. Tap Internet Email Account.

8. Enter your email address and password.

9. Tap Next.

10. Tap Internet Email Account.

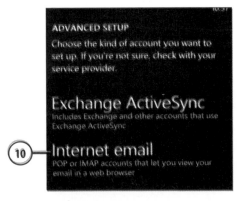

11. Enter your name into the Account Name field.

12. Enter your name (as you would like it to be displayed to recipients) into the Your Name field.

13. Enter your server's Fully Qualified Domain Name (FQDN) or IP address into the Incoming Email Server field.

14. Tap the Account Type field and choose either POP3 or IMAP4.

15. Type the login name for your Windows domain into the User Name field. This name must be entered either as an email address or in domain\username format.

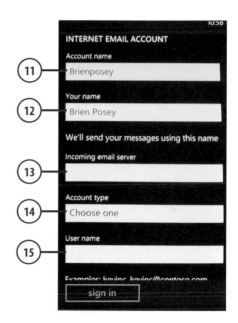

16. If the outgoing server requires authentication, select the Outgoing Server Requires Authentication check box and the Use the Same User Name and Password For Sending Email check box.

17. Depending on your mail server's configuration, you might also need to enable SSL encryption. If so, then tap the Advanced Settings button and select the Require SSL for Incoming Mail and the Require SSL for Outgoing Mail check boxes.

18. Tap Sign In.

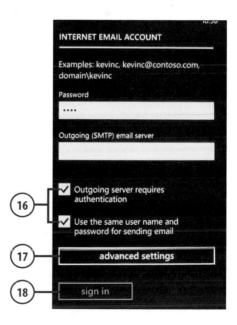

Go Further

ADVANCED SETTINGS

The Advanced Settings screen can also be used to control how frequently Windows checks for new mail. The default option is to check for new mail every two hours. Checking more frequently can impact battery life and can also result in higher cellular bills if you do not have an unlimited data plan.

The Advanced Settings screen also offers an option to control how much mail history is stored on the phone. By default all of the mail from the last two weeks is stored on the phone, but you can store more or less mail as your needs dictate. This option only effects the phone's storage, not your actual mailbox.

Microsoft Outlook Mobile

Regardless of whether you get your mail from Windows Live, Exchange Server, Gmail, or something else, all of the mail is made accessible through Microsoft Outlook Mobile. The techniques discussed in this section are valid regardless of what type of mailbox you are accessing.

Accessing Your Mailbox

For every mail account that you set up, Windows Phone creates a separate smart tile on the Start screen. For example, if you set up a Windows Live account and an Exchange Server account, you will have a live tile for each. The live tile displays the name of the mailbox and the number of unread messages that are waiting for you. In addition, you can find links to each of your mail accounts within the App List.

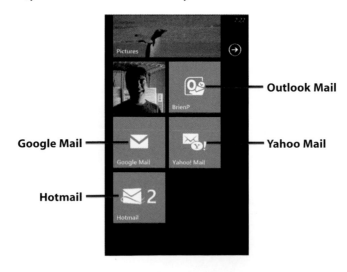

Outlook Mail

Google Mail

Yahoo Mail

Hotmail

The Outlook Mobile Interface

When you tap a link to one of your mailboxes, Outlook Mobile opens. The main Outlook Mobile screen contains several different objects including those shown here.

A. **The current time**.

B. **The name of the mailbox you are currently using**—It is important to verify the mailbox that you are connected to because Windows Phone can be connected to multiple mailboxes simultaneously.

C. **The current view of your messages**—All is selected by default, but you can flick the View option to view unread messages, flagged messages, or urgent messages.

D. **Your Mail**—Outlook Mobile displays all of the messages in the current folder.

E. **The New icon**—Tap this icon to compose a new message.

F. **The Select icon**—Tap this icon to access a screen that lets you perform bulk operations on your messages.

G. **The Sync icon**—Tap this icon to manually check for new mail

H. **The Search icon**—Tap this icon to search your mail.

I. **The Menu icon**—Flick this icon upward to reveal the menu.

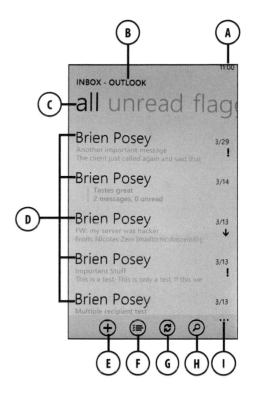

The Anatomy of a Message

When you open Outlook Mobile, you will see the messages in your Inbox. Several pieces of information are listed for each message:

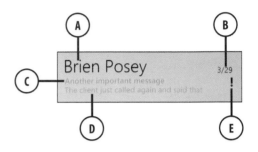

A. **The Sender**—This is the name of the person who sent the message.

B. **The Timestamp**—When the message arrived.

C. **The Subject Line**—The subject line is displayed in blue if the message is unread. Otherwise it is shown in black.

D. **Message Preview**—The first several words of the message are displayed beneath the subject line.

E. **Flag**—The optional flag indicates whether a message is important, unimportant, flagged for follow up, complete, or if the message contains an attachment.

Opening a Message

You can view a message by simply tapping it.

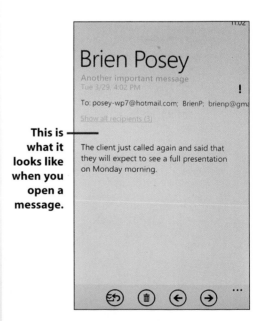

This is what it looks like when you open a message.

Opening an Attachment

If a message contains an attachment, you can view it by following these steps:

1. Tap the message to open it.

2. Tap the attachment to open it.

3. Windows Phone automatically opens the application associated with the attachment file type (assuming that such an application is installed on the phone).

Trouble Opening Attachments

Although it might be somewhat counterintuitive, you can only open attachments by tapping them. If you accidentally double tap an attachment, it won't open. Double tapping an attachment is essentially the same as canceling the download. Incidentally, attachment downloads can take a while to complete, so the attachments might not open immediately.

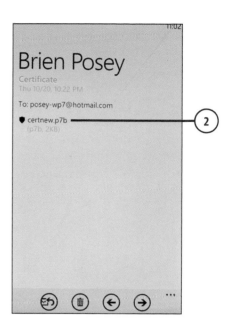

Replying to a Message

To reply to a message

1. Tap the message to open it.

2. Tap the Respond icon.

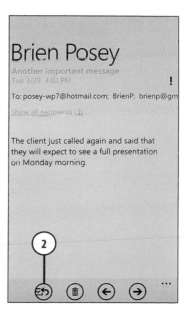

3. Tap Reply.

4. Compose your response.

5. Tap the Send icon.

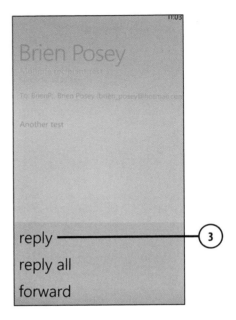

Replying to Multiple Recipients

1. Tap the message to open it.

2. Tap the Respond icon.

3. Tap Reply All.

4. Compose your response.

5. Tap the Send icon.

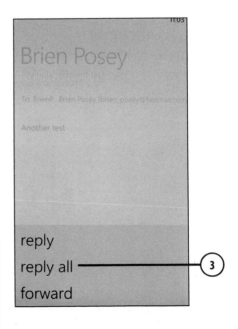

Forwarding a Message

1. Tap the message to open it.
2. Tap the Reply icon.
3. Tap Forward.
4. Compose your response.
5. Tap the Send button.

Viewing New Mail

You can tell the difference between new mail (unread messages) and old mail (messages that have already been read) by looking at the color of the subject line. Outlook displays the subject line of new messages in blue, and the subject line is shown in black for old messages. If you would like to temporarily see only the new messages in your mailbox, you can do so by following these steps:

1. Open your mailbox.

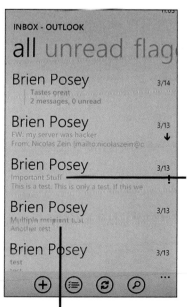

A new message's subject line is displayed in blue.

An old message's subject line is displayed in black.

2. Flick the view setting from All to Unread.

3. To return the view to normal when you are done, flick the view from Unread to All.

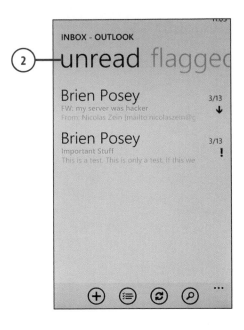

Viewing Urgent Mail

When you receive an urgent message, Windows Phone displays a red exclamation point alongside the message to indicate the message is important. However, Outlook Mobile also has an option for viewing only the most important messages. To do so

1. Open your mailbox.

2. Flick the View setting from All to Urgent.

3. When you are done, you can return the mailbox to its previous state by flicking the view setting from Urgent to All.

Urgent messages are flagged with an exclamation point icon.

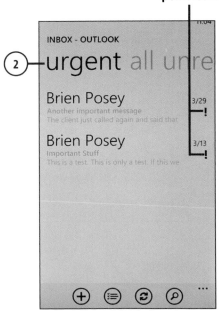

Deleting a Message

To delete a message without opening it:

1. Tap and hold the message.

2. When the menu appears, tap
   Delete.

To delete a message that is open, tap
the Delete icon.

A Word of Caution

You should exercise caution when
deleting messages because neither of the methods mentioned
here ask for confirmation prior to
deleting a message.

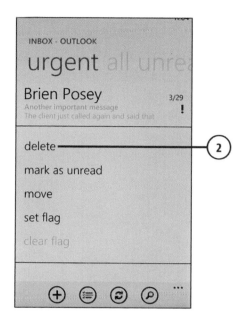

**You can delete a message by
tapping the Delete icon.**

Bulk Delete

If you need to delete more than one or two messages, you should perform a bulk delete. To do so

1. Go to the Inbox.

2. Tap the Select icon.

3. Select the check boxes corresponding to the messages you want to delete.

4. Tap the Delete icon.

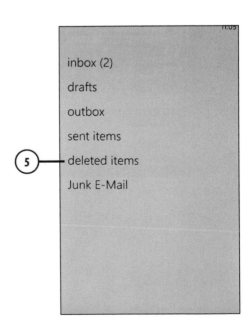

Recovering a Deleted Message

If you accidentally delete a message, you can recover it from the Deleted Items folder. To do so, follow these steps:

1. Open your mailbox.

2. Flick the ... icon upward to reveal the submenu.

3. Tap the Folders option.

4. Tap Show All Folders.

5. Tap Deleted Items.

6. Tap and hold the message you want to recover.

7. Tap Move.

8. Tap Inbox.

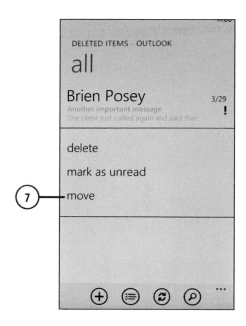

Marking a Message as Read

To mark a message as Read

1. Tap and hold the message.

2. Tap Mark as Read.

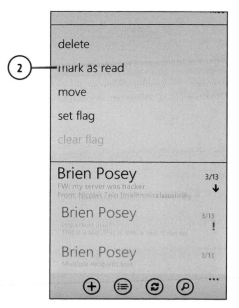

Marking a Message as Unread

To mark a message as Unread

1. Tap and hold the message.

2. Tap Mark as Unread.

Marking Multiple Messages as Read or Unread

The method just discussed works well for dealing with individual messages, but there is an easier way to mark multiple messages as Read or Unread. To do so

1. Go to the Inbox or to the folder containing the messages you want to manage.

2. Tap the Select icon.

3. Select the check boxes corresponding to the messages you want to flag or unflag.

4. Flick the ... icon upward to reveal the menu beneath the icons that are found at the bottom of the screen.

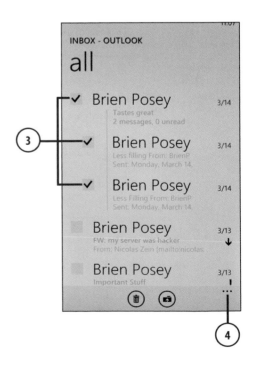

5. Tap either Mark as Read or Mark as Unread.

Moving a Message

Windows Phone allows you to move messages into folders for long-term retention. If you need to move a message into a folder, you can accomplish the task by following these steps:

1. Tap and hold the message.

2. Tap Move.

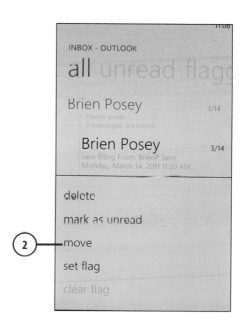

3. Tap the folder you want to move
   the message into.

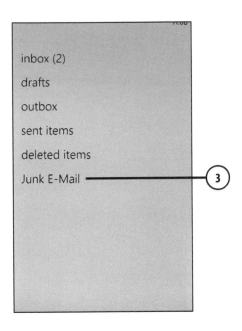

Performing a Bulk Move

If you need to move more than one
message to another folder, you
should perform a bulk move. To do so

1. Go to the Inbox or to the folder
   containing the messages you
   want to move.

2. Tap the Select icon.

3. Select the check boxes corresponding to the messages you want to
   move. All of the messages you
   select should be destined for the
   same folder.

4. Tap the Move icon.

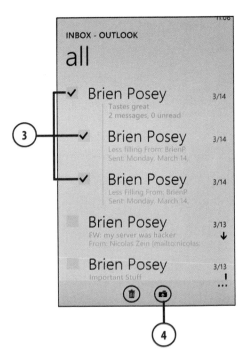

5. Tap the folder you want to move the selected messages into.

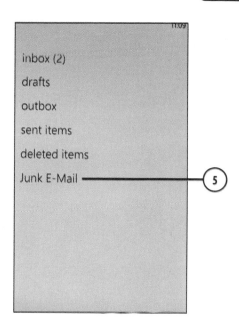

Viewing Folders

Windows Phone displays the Inbox folder by default, but you can view any of your mailbox folders. To do so

1. Open the mailbox.

2. Flick the ... icon upward to reveal the submenu.

3. Tap Folders.

4. Tap Show All Folders.

5. Tap the folder you want to view.

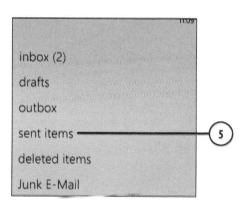

Empty Folders

When you view a folder, the folder might at first appear empty. In an effort to save space on the phone, Microsoft does not automatically synchronize all folders. For example, it would normally be a waste of space and bandwidth to synchronize the junk mail folder. If you need to view the contents of a folder that initially appears to be empty, open the folder and then tap Sync This Folder.

Flagging a Message

Windows Phone offers full support for message flags. To flag a message:

1. Tap and hold the message.
2. Tap Set Flag.

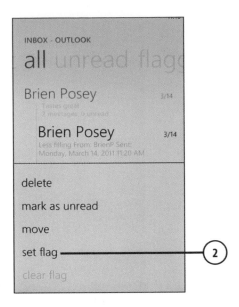

It's Not All Good

Flagging messages seems to only be supported for Exchange Server mailboxes. The flagging option is missing from other types of mailboxes, including Microsoft Live.

Clearing a Message Flag

To clear the flag from a message

1. Tap and hold the message.
2. Tap Clear Flag.

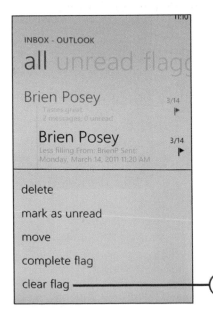

Viewing Flagged Messages

You can easily locate flagged messages by switching to the Flagged view:

1. Go to the Inbox or to the folder containing the flagged messages.

2. Flick the screen to access the Flagged view.

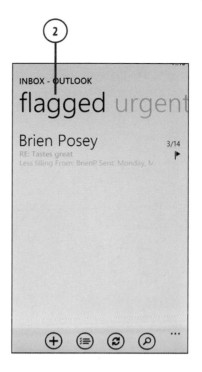

Flagging or Unflagging Multiple Messages

To flag or unflag multiple messages

1. Go to the Inbox or to the folder containing the messages you want to manage.

2. Tap the Select icon.

3. Select the check boxes corresponding to the messages you want to flag or unflag.

4. Flick the ... icon upward to reveal the menu beneath the icons that are found at the bottom of the screen.

5. Tap either Set Flag or Clear Flag.

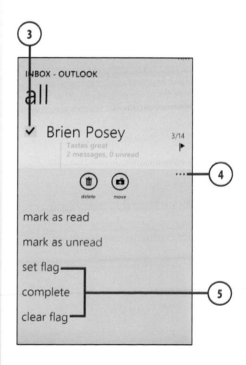

Marking a Message as Complete

Just as you can flag a message, you can mark a message as complete:

1. Go to the Inbox or to the folder containing the messages you want to manage.

2. Tap the Select icon.

3. Select the check boxes corresponding to the messages you want to mark.

4. Flick the ... icon upward to reveal the menu beneath the icons found at the bottom of the screen.

5. Tap Complete.

Accidental Completion
If you accidentally flag a message as complete, you can get rid of the flag by using the Clear Flag option just discussed.

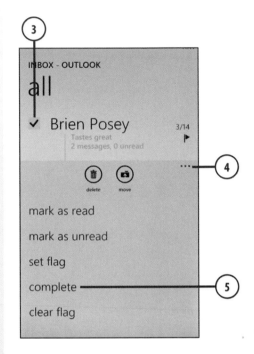

Composing a New Message

One of the most basic messaging tasks is to compose a new message. The message composition screen contains several elements including

A. **The current time**.

B. **To Field**—This is where you enter the recipient's email address.

C. **Add Contact icon**.

D. **Subject Line**—This is where you type the message's subject.

E. **Message Body Section**—This is where you actually compose your message.

F. **Send icon**—Tap this icon to send the message.

G. **Attach Icon**—Tap this icon to add an attachment to the message.

H. **Close Icon**—Tap this icon to cancel the message rather than send it.

I. **Submenu Icon**—Flick this icon upward to access a submenu with access to the CC, Blind CC, and Priority options.

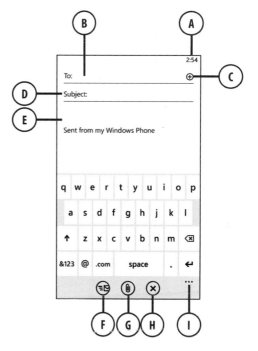

You can compose a new message by following these steps:

1. Open your mailbox.

2. Tap the New Message icon.

3. Tap the To field and then enter the address to which you want to send the message.

4. Tap the Subject field.

5. Enter a subject line for the message.

6. Tap the message body.

7. Compose your message.

8. Tap the Send icon.

SENDING MAIL TO YOUR CONTACTS

The instructions just described assume you are going to be manually entering the message recipient's email address. However, Windows Phone gives you the option of sending an email directly to one of your contacts by tapping the Add Contact icon. There are also other methods of sending messages to your contacts, which is discussed in the section on the People Hub in Chapter 5, "Windows Phone 7 Apps."

Go Further

Canceling a New Message

Occasionally, you might begin composing a message and then change your mind about sending it. When this happens you can cancel the message by performing these steps:

1. Tap the Close icon.

2. If you have not yet entered any information for the new message, the message will be canceled with no further questions. Otherwise, you will see a menu with the following choices:

   A. **Save**—The message is not sent, but it is saved in your Drafts folder so that you can edit and send the message at a later time.

   B. **Delete**—The message is deleted without saving a draft copy.

The Back Button

If you tap the Back button while composing a message, Windows Phone displays the menu just shown rather than immediately navigating away from the message (unless the new message is completely empty).

Adding Message Attachments

Windows Phone allows you to send photographs as message attachments. You have the option of sending a photograph either from your Camera Roll or directly from the built-in camera.

Sending Pictures From Your Photo Roll

To send a picture from your Photo Roll, complete the following steps:

1. Begin composing a new message.

2. Tap the Attachment icon.

3. Tap the Camera Roll icon or click the album containing the image that you want to send.

4. Tap the photo you want to send.

5. You are returned to the message composition screen. Finish composing your message (if necessary).

6. Tap the Send icon.

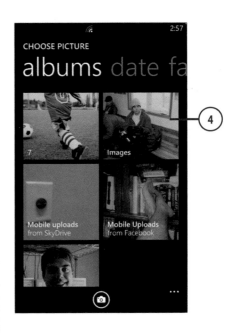

Multiple Attachments

You can add multiple attachments to an email message, but you must select each attachment separately.

Sending a Picture From the Camera

Windows Phone allows you to access the camera from directly within the message composition screen and email a photo immediately after snapping it. To do so, follow these steps:

1. Begin composing a new message.

2. Tap the Attachment icon.

3. Tap the Camera icon.

4. Press the Camera button to snap a picture.

5. If you are satisfied with the way the picture looks, tap Accept. Otherwise tap Retake.

6. You are returned to the message composition screen, and the new picture is added as an attachment. It is worth noting that this picture will not be added to the Camera Roll.

It's Not All Good

Although the message composition screen contains an attachments icon, the only type of attachments that you are allowed to add to messages are photographs. Windows Phone does allow you to send other types of files as e-mail attachments, but you must do so through the application that created the file. For example, if you want to send someone a Microsoft Word document, you have to do so through Microsoft Word Mobile. This option is discussed in more detail in Chapter 6, "Microsoft Office Mobile."

Removing a Message Attachment

When you add an attachment to a message, you have the option of removing the attachment prior to sending the message. To do so, follow these steps:

1. Tap the Remove link, which is located just beneath the attachment.

2. When Windows asks if you want to remove the attachment, tap Yes.

Setting Message Priority

When you compose a new message, you have the option of setting the message's priority to High, Normal, or Low. To set the priority for a message, follow these steps:

1. From the message composition screen, flick the ... icon upward to reveal the submenu.

2. Tap Priority.

3. Tap either High, Normal, or Low.

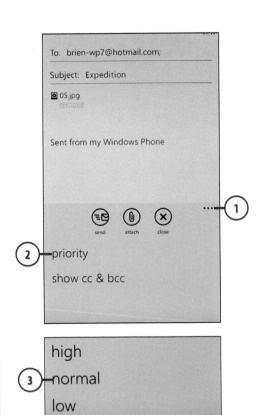

Go Further

VERIFYING THE MESSAGE PRIORITY

When you set a message's priority, Windows does not provide you with any kind of message telling you that the priority has been set. To verify the message priority, you must look for a flag in the upper right portion of the message composition screen. You have to scroll all the way to the top of the screen to see this flag. Priority flags are only displayed for High and Low priority messages. Messages with a Normal priority do not contain priority flags.

CC and Blind CC

Windows Phone gives you the option of copying or blindly copying other recipients on a message. To do so, follow these steps:

1. From the message composition screen, flick the ... icon upward to access the submenu.

2. Tap Show CC and BCC.

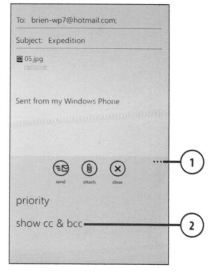

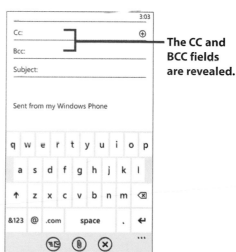

The CC and BCC fields are revealed.

Checking for New Mail

Depending on the type of mailbox you are connected to, new messages might not show up in your Inbox immediately. You can manually check for new messages by doing the following:

1. Open the mailbox that you want to check.

2. Tap the Sync icon.

Removing Mail Accounts

If you no longer need mobile access to a mail account, you can easily remove the account without affecting any of the other mail accounts that might be set up on the phone. To remove a mail account, complete these steps:

1. Press the Start button.

2. Flick the arrow icon to access the App List.

3. Scroll to the bottom of the App List and tap Settings.

4. Tap Email + Account.

5. Tap and hold the account you want to delete.

6. When the menu appears, tap Delete.

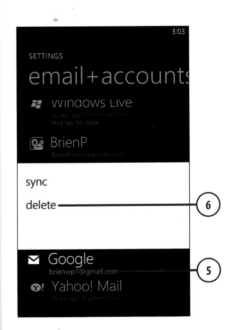

7. You will see a warning message indicating that you are about to delete all of the information associated with the account. Tap the Delete key to remove the account.

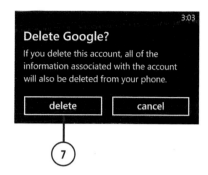

3:03

Delete Google?

If you delete this account, all of the information associated with the account will also be deleted from your phone.

| delete | cancel |

⑦

REMOVING MICROSOFT LIVE ACCOUNTS

GoFurther

Because Microsoft Live accounts are used for more than just email access, Windows Phone does not allow you to remove them in the manner just described. If you want to remove a Windows Live account, you will have to reset the phone.

Linking Mailboxes

Although Windows Phone supports the use of multiple mailboxes, some people prefer to access all of their mail through a single mailbox. This can be accomplished through mailbox linking. When you link mailboxes, all of the mail from those mailboxes is displayed as if it existed in a single mailbox. To link mailboxes, follow these steps:

1. Open your main mailbox.

2. Flick the ... icon upward to reveal the shortcut menu.

3. Tap Linked Inboxes.

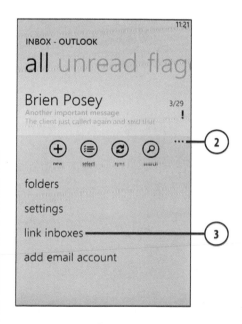

11:21

INBOX - OUTLOOK

all unread flag

Brien Posey 3/29
Another important message
The client just called again and said that !

⊕ ⊜ ↻ ⊘ ··· ②
new   select   sync   search

folders

settings

link inboxes ——— ③

add email account

4. Tap the name of the mailbox you want to link.

5. Tap Rename Linked Inbox.

6. Give your Inbox a name that reflects its purpose.

7. Tap the Done icon.

8. The linked mailbox is displayed on the Start screen. Multiple mailbox icons designate it as a collection of linked mailboxes.

This is a linked mailbox.

Unlinking Inboxes

If you later decide you want to unlink your mailboxes, you can easily do so. To unlink a mailbox, follow these steps:

1. Open your linked mailbox.

2. Flick the ... icon upward to reveal the shortcut menu.

3. Tap Linked Inboxes.

4. Tap the name of the mailbox you want to unlink.

5. Tap the Unlink button.

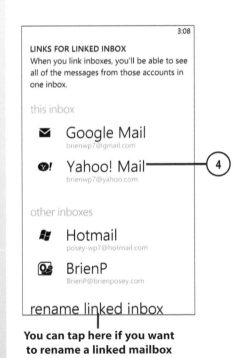

You can tap here if you want to rename a linked mailbox

Conversation View

By default, Windows Phone groups messages into conversation view. Conversation view reduces clutter in your mailbox by grouping messages from each sender into a dedicated container. If you want to disable Conversation view, follow these steps:

1. Open your Inbox.

2. Flick the ... icon upward to reveal the submenu.

3. Tap Settings.

4. Set the Conversation slidebar to Off.

You can re-enable conversation view by setting the slidebar to On.

Message Signatures

By default Windows Phone devices add the phrase "Sent from my Windows Phone" to the end of each message you send. However, you can turn this signature off or customize it. To do so, follow these steps:

1. Open your Inbox.

2. Flick the ... icon upward to reveal the submenu.

3. Tap Settings.

4. If you want to customize the signature, tap it and type a new signature.

5. If you want to disable the signature, set the Signature slidebar to Off.

6. Tap the Done icon.

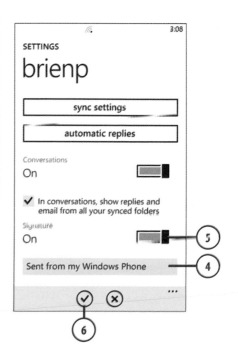

Blind CCing Yourself

Some people like to send a copy to themselves of every message they send. Windows Phone includes an automatic BCC option. If you want to always BCC yourself, you can do so by following these steps:

1. Open your Inbox.

2. Flick the ... icon upward to reveal the submenu.

3. Tap Settings.

4. Select the Always BCC Myself check box.

5. Tap the Done icon.

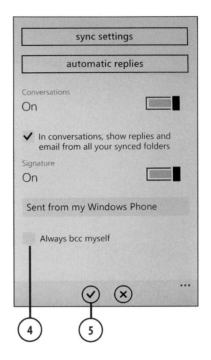

You can access your music
collection through your
Windows Phone 7 device.

In the first chapter you learned how to install the Zune software onto your PC. In this chapter you learn how to begin using the software to enable your phone to play music and movies.

4

The Multimedia Experience

The Summary Screen

When you initially open the Zune software, the summary screen is displayed. The Summary screen confirms that your phone is connected to the PC and shows you how much storage space is available on the phone.

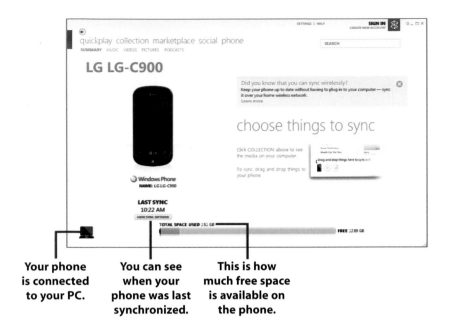

Your phone is connected to your PC.

You can see when your phone was last synchronized.

This is how much free space is available on the phone.

Setting Up a Zune Account

Even though you don't need a Zune account for adding items from your collection to your phone, a Zune account is required for downloading items from the marketplace. If you want to set up a Zune account, complete these steps:

1. Open the Zune software.

2. Click Sign In.

3. When prompted, enter your Windows Live ID and password.

4. You now see a message indicating that some additional information must be collected. Click Next to clear this message.

5. When prompted, enter your country, language, postal code, and birthdate.

6. Click I Accept to accept the Terms of Service.

7. The next screen asks you if you want to join Zune Social. You have three options:

   A. **Share With Everyone**—Your Zune Profile, Friends List, Zune Activities, and the content you have played is shared with the world.

   B. **Share With My Friends Only**—Your friends are able to view your Zune Profile, friends list, Zune activities, and recently played content.

   C. **Don't Share**—Your information is kept private.

8. Decide whether or not you want to receive Zune Communications (Zune newsletters and artist and music recommendations) and either select or deselect the Zune Communications check box accordingly.

9. Determine whether or not you want to personalize your Zune experience. If you choose to personalize your experience, information about your recently played content and your content ratings are sent to Microsoft and used to tailor the Zune music experience to match your interests.

10. Click Next.

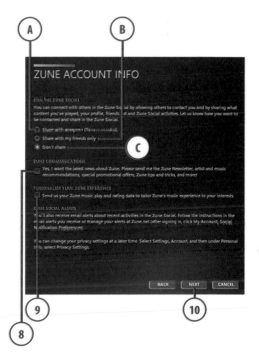

11. Provide the software with a Zune
    Tag. A Zune Tag is a name that
    represents your identity in the
    Zune social network. Your tag
    appears in the Zune software and
    on your Zune card.

12. Click Next.

13. Click Finish.

Managing Your Collection

The primary method for making music, videos, pictures, and podcasts available on your phone involves copying (syncing) items from your collection to the phone. In Zune speak, the collection refers to all of your multimedia content, which exists by default within your Windows profile (C:\Users\<your name>) and the public profile (C:\Users\Public). Although these are the default locations used within the collection, you can modify the collection to use custom paths. This is particularly useful when you store music, videos, or pictures in nondefault locations, such as on a network storage device.

You can access the collection paths by completing these steps:

1. Open the Zune software.

2. Click Collection.

3. Click Settings.

4. Verify that the Collection option is selected.

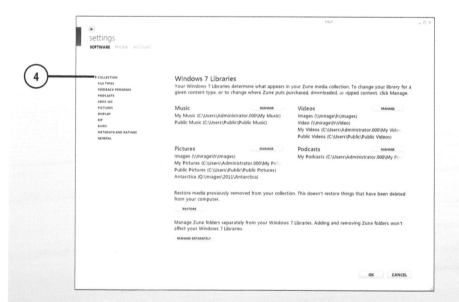

As you can see in the figure, the Zune software maintains a separate set of collection paths for music, videos, pictures, and podcasts. You can modify the paths used by the collection for an individual data type by clicking the

Manage button that is associated with that data type. After doing so, you can click the Add button to add additional paths to the collection, or you can click a path and then click the Remove button to remove it from the collection.

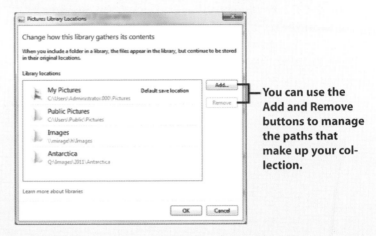

You can use the Add and Remove buttons to manage the paths that make up your collection.

Adding Music to Your Phone

The easiest way to add music to your phone is to simply drag and drop items from your music collection.

1. Open the Zune software.

2. Click Collection.

3. Click Music.

4. Drag a song, album, artist, or even an entire genre to the phone icon in the lower left corner of the interface.

Adding Videos to Your Phone

Videos can be added to the phone in much the same way as you add music. To add a video to your phone, follow these steps:

1. Open the Zune software.

2. Click Collection.

3. Click Videos.

4. Drag videos from your collection to the phone icon in the lower left corner of the window.

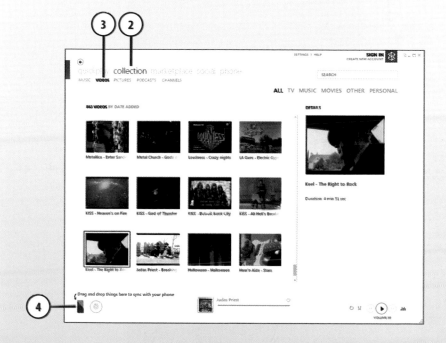

Adding Pictures to Your Phone

1. Open the Zune software.

2. Click Collection.

3. Click Pictures.

4. Navigate through your photo collection to locate the pictures you want to put on the phone.

5. Drag the desired pictures to the phone icon in the lower left corner of the window.

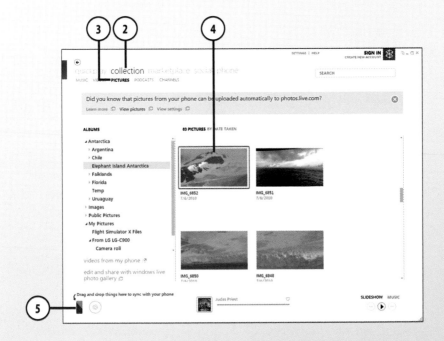

Adding Podcasts to Your Phone

Just as Windows Phone supports playing music and videos, it also offers built-in support for podcasts. To add a podcast to your phone, follow these steps:

1. Open the Zune software.

2. Click Collection.

3. Click Podcasts.

4. Drag the desired podcast to the phone icon in the lower left corner of the window.

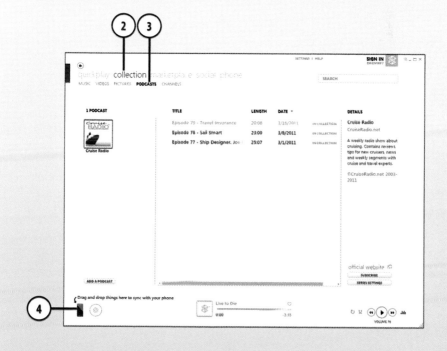

Getting Podcasts from the Marketplace

A huge variety of podcasts is available through the Marketplace. To subscribe to podcasts through the Marketplace, follow these steps:

1. Open the Zune software.

2. Click Marketplace.

3. Click Podcasts.

4. Click a podcast genre (or click one of the recommended podcasts).

5. Click the podcast you want to subscribe to.

6. Click Subscribe. The podcasts are automatically downloaded to the Zune software.

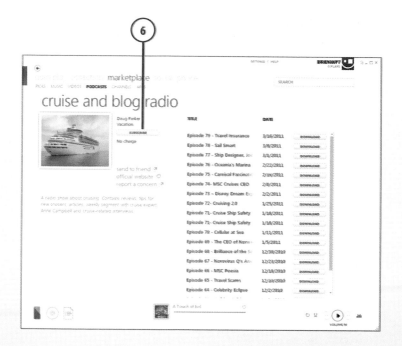

Managing Podcast Subscriptions

When you look at your collection of podcasts, you might discover that not all of the podcasts are immediately available to play or to synchronize with your phone. For example, in the next figure, only the first three podcasts are currently saved on the PC. By default, the Zune software downloads the three most recent podcasts in a series but does not attempt to automatically download the entire series. If you would like to listen to other podcasts in the series, you can either click the Download button for the podcast you want to listen to, or you can modify your subscription settings. It is also possible to download individual podcasts by clicking the Download button rather than subscribing to a podcast.

To change the subscription settings for a podcast, perform these steps:

1. Open the Zune software.

2. Click Collection.

3. Click Podcasts.

4. Click the podcast subscription you want to manage.

5. Click the Series Settings button.

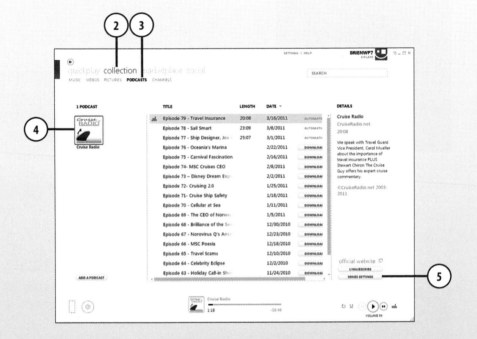

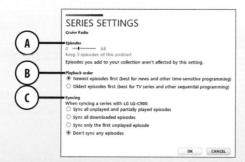

SERIES SETTINGS

Cruise Radio

A — Episodes
0 ——•——— All
Keep 3 episodes of this podcast
Episodes you add to your collection aren't affected by this setting.

B — Playback order
⦿ Newest episodes first (best for news and other time-sensitive programming)
○ Oldest episodes first (best for TV series and other sequential programming)

C — Syncing
When syncing a series with LG LG-C900:
○ Sync all unplayed and partially played episodes
○ Sync all downloaded episodes
○ Sync only the first unplayed episode
⦿ Don't sync any episodes

[OK] [CANCEL]

6. Configure the series settings for your podcast. You have the following options:

A. **Episodes**—The Episodes slidebar allows you to control how many podcast episodes to keep. This setting only controls the number of podcast episodes that are automatically downloaded and retained. By default, the three most recent episodes are downloaded and retained. When a new episode comes out, the oldest episode is deleted. However, episodes are not deleted if you have added them to your collection.

B. **Playback Order**—You can choose to play either the newest episodes first or the oldest episodes first. Playing the oldest episodes first is the best option for fictional shows with ongoing plots. Playing the newest episode first is best for podcasts containing timely information (such as news programs).

C. **Syncing**—The Zune software gives you several options for syncing podcasts with your phone. You can sync all unplayed (and partially played) episodes, all downloaded episodes, only the first unplayed episode, or you can choose not to sync podcasts with the phone.

Playing a Podcast Through the Phone

To play a podcast, follow these steps:

1. Press the Start button.

2. Tap Music + Videos.

3. Tap Podcasts.

4. Tap the podcast you want to play. It is worth noting that the Podcast screen is divided into an Audio and a Video page. You can flick to the Video page to play video podcasts.

We Now Return to the Program Already In Progress

If you begin playing a podcast on your computer (through the Zune software), and then part of the way through the podcast you decide to synchronize it to the phone, you will find that when you play the podcast through the phone, it begins playing at the point where you left off playing it on your computer. Of course, you can always rewind the podcast if you choose to.

Audio Podcasts | **Video Podcasts**

Unsubscribing from a Podcast

You can unsubscribe a podcast at any time by following these steps:

1. Open the Zune software.

2. Click Collection.

3. Click Podcasts.

4. Click the podcast you want to unsubscribe to.

5. Click the Unsubscribe button.

6. To save the podcast for which episodes that have already been downloaded, click Save. Otherwise click Delete.

Click Save to keep the podcasts that you have already downloaded.

Click Delete to delete the existing podcasts.

Configuring Sync Options

Depending on how large your collection of music, videos, pictures, and podcasts is, you might opt to synchronize your entire collection to your phone, or you might prefer to be more selective about which content gets synced. You can control how content is synchronized by editing the Sync Options. To do so, follow these steps:

1. Plug your phone into your computer with the USB cable.

2. When the Zune software opens, click Phone.

3. Click the View Sync Options button.

4. Choose Your Sync Settings.

    You can set the sync options separately for music, videos, pictures, and podcasts. For each category you have the following options:

    *   **All**—Synchronize all media in the category (all music, all pictures, and so on).

    *   **Items I Choose**—Only items you drag and drop to the phone are synchronized. A separate sync group is created for each item. Sync groups are discussed in the next section.

    *   **Manual Sync**—Manual sync is similar to Items I Choose except that unwanted items must be deleted manually.

>>> Go Further

SAVING STORAGE SPACE

You can save storage space on your phone by selecting the option not to sync songs with the broken heart rating. Zune allows you to rate songs based on how much you like them, and the broken heart rating is reserved for songs that you do not like. Therefore, if you choose not to synchronize songs with the broken heart rating, you can conserve storage space by not filling up your phone with songs you don't even like.

Sync Groups

As you begin adding multimedia content to your phone, Windows automatically creates a sync group for each content type. Simply put, a sync group is a list of content that is to be synchronized to the phone.

Although the Zune software creates sync groups automatically for each piece of content you synchronize, you can also create dynamic sync groups. The advantage of doing so is that you can synchronize content to your phone based on a set of preferences rather than having to manually drag and drop individual items.

Viewing Existing Sync Groups

To see the existing sync groups, follow these steps:

1. Open the Zune software.

2. Click Phone.

3. Click Settings.

4. Click Sync Groups.

5. Click the Expand button that corresponds to your preferred content type to reveal the existing sync groups.

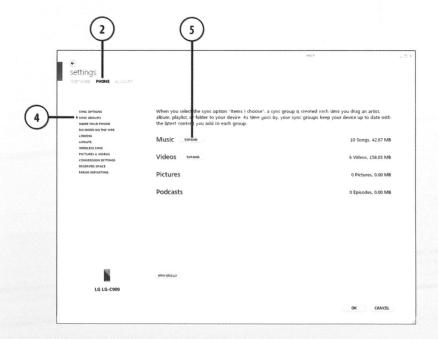

Sync Groups

In the figure just shown, each sync group represents a piece of content that was manually synchronized with the phone. You will notice that in the Music section there is a single sync group, which corresponds to the Painkiller album. If songs had been synced individually, there would have been a separate sync group for each song rather than a single sync group for the album. Likewise, in the Videos section there is a separate sync group for each video because the videos were added individually.

Creating a Dynamic Sync Group

Although the Zune software creates sync groups automatically, you can create dynamic sync groups that are based on one or more rules. For example, suppose you wanted to create a sync group of hard rock/heavy metal music from the years 1984 to 1986. To do so, you would follow these steps:

1. Open the Zune software.

2. Click Phone.

3. Click Settings.

4. Click Sync Groups.

5. Click New Group.

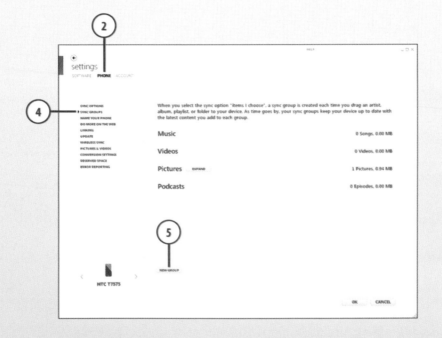

6. Enter a name for your sync group.

7. Set the source to My Music Collection.

8. Set the Album Artists to All.

9. Set the Composer to All.

10. Set the Genre to Include Heavy Metal.

11. Set the Genre to Include Rock (this causes the rule to look for both Heavy Metal and Rock).

12. Set the Filters option to One or More Filters.

13. Set the Year option to 1984 to 1986.

14. Click OK.

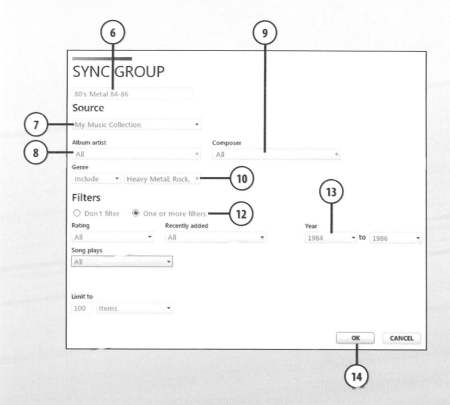

15. After clicking OK, the sync process begins.

The sync process begins.

16. You can view the contents of the new sync group by clicking the Expand button beneath Just Added to Phone.

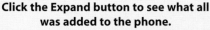

Click the Expand button to see what all was added to the phone.

Removing Synchronized Content

Removing synchronized content from the phone is a matter of deleting the corresponding sync group. To get rid of a sync group, perform these steps:

1. Open the Zune software.

2. Click Phone.

3. Click Settings.

4. Click Sync Groups.

5. Click the Expand button for the Sync Group you want to remove.

6. Click the Remove Group button that corresponds to the Sync Group you want to delete.

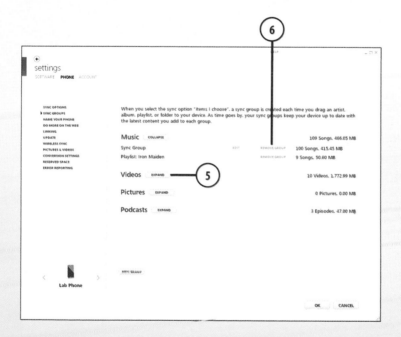

7. When you see the Remove Sync Group dialog box, click OK

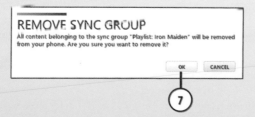

Wirelessly Syncing Your Phone

Although the previous sections have instructed you to synchronize content with your phone by plugging the phone into your computer and dragging and dropping the media you want to synchronize, connecting the phone to the computer's USB port is optional. As an alternative, you can perform a wireless synchronization over a Wi-Fi network. To do so, complete these steps:

1. Verify your phone is configured to use Wi-Fi connectivity.

2. Plug your phone into your computer using the USB cable.

3. Open the Zune software.

4. Click Phone.

5. Click Settings.

6. Click Wireless Sync.

7. Verify that the Wireless Sync screen shows the phone connected to the correct Wi-Fi network.

8. Click the Set Up Wireless Sync button.

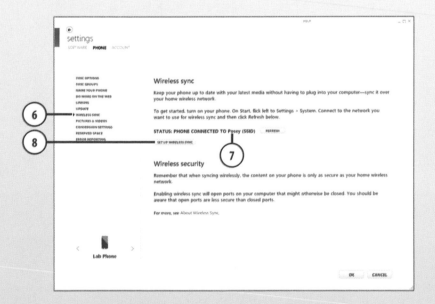

9. Confirm your wireless network and click Next.

10. When the wireless sync completes, click Done. The Zune software verifies that wireless sync is enabled.

11. Verify that the Zune software reports that the Wireless Sync is enabled and click OK.

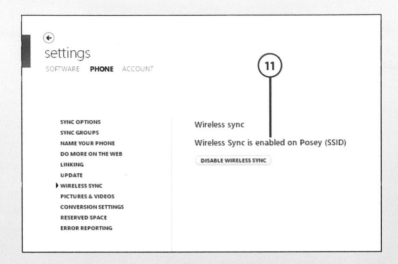

Playing Music Through the Phone

When you have synchronized music to the phone, you can play it. The phone gives you several different options for playing music. For example, you can play individual songs, an entire album, all of the songs by a particular artist, or even all of the songs from a certain genre.

Playing Songs

If you want to play an individual song, you can do so by following these steps:

1. Press the Start button.

2. Tap Music + Video.

3. Flick the Music + Video Screen to access the Zune page.

4. Tap Music.

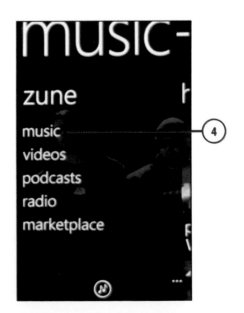

5. Flick to Songs.

6. Tap the song you want to play.

7. The song plays.

The Play Screen

The Play screen contains several elements including

A. The name of the artist.

B. The name of the album that the song is from.

C. The album art.

D. The time line, which shows the length of the song and how far into the song you are.

E. The name of the song.

F. The next two songs that will be played.

G. The Rewind Button—Pressing this button once restarts the song. Pressing it twice plays the next song.

H. The Pause button.

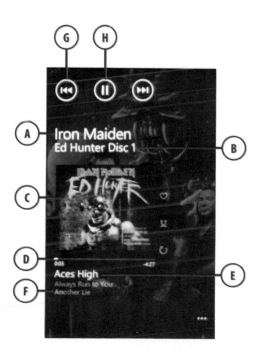

I. The fast forward button—Pressing the button once fast forwards the song. Pressing it twice starts the next song.

J. Rate—Tapping this icon so that the heart is colored in indicates that you like this song. Tapping the icon again turns the icon into a broken heart indicating that you do not like the song. A heart with a black center like the one in the figure indicates that the song is unrated. You can also rate music in the same way through the Zune software.

K. Shuffle—This icon causes the phone to play music in a random order.

L. Repeat—The song will play repeatedly.

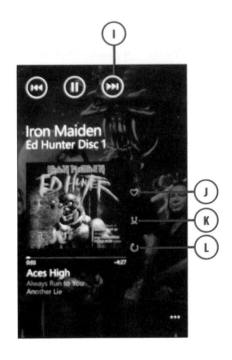

Playing an Album

Just as you can play an individual song, you can also play an entire album. To do so, complete these steps:

1. Press the Start button.

2. Tap Music + Video.

3. Flick the Music + Video Screen to access the Zune page.

4. Tap Music.

5. Flick to Albums.

6. Tap the album you want to play.

7. The album begins to play.

Playing a Music Genre

If you would like to hear all of the songs on your phone that belong to a certain genre, complete these steps:

1. Press the Start button.

2. Tap Music + Video.

3. Flick the Music + Video Screen to access the Zune page.

4. Tap Music.

5. Flick to Genres.

6. Tap the genre you want to play.

7. The phone begins playing all of the songs from that genre.

Playing a Specific Artist

Windows Phone also allows you to play songs from a certain artist, even if those songs span multiple albums. To do so, follow these steps:

1. Press the Start button.

2. Tap Music + Video.

3. Flick the Music + Video Screen to access the Zune page.

4. Tap Music.

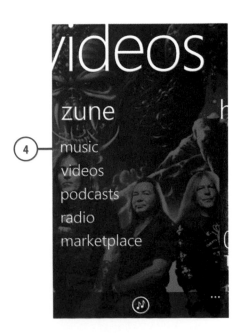

5. Flick to Artists.

6. Tap the artist whose songs you want to play.

7. The phone begins playing all of the songs from the selected artist.

Play Lists

Another option for playing music with your phone involves using playlists. A playlist is a list of songs that are played in sequential order (kind of like a mix tape).

Creating a Play List

You can create a playlist through the Zune software. If you have previously created playlists through Windows Media Player, those playlists should also be available to you through the Zune software. You can create a playlist by following these steps:

1. Open the Zune software.

2. Click Collection.

3. Click Music.

4. Click Playlists.

5. Click New Playlist.

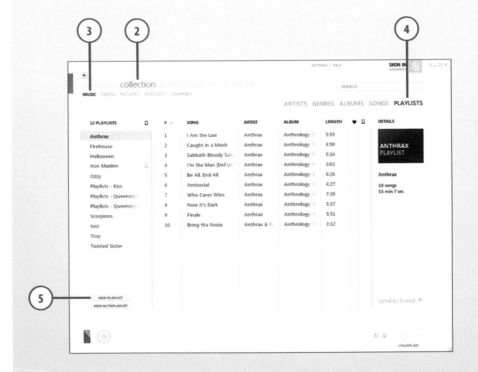

6. Enter a name for your new playlist and click OK.

7. Click Artists.

8. Locate the first song that you want to add to the playlist.

9. Drag the song to the playlist icon.

10. Repeat the process for each additional song you want to add.

11. When you are done, click Playlists to confirm that your tracks have been added.

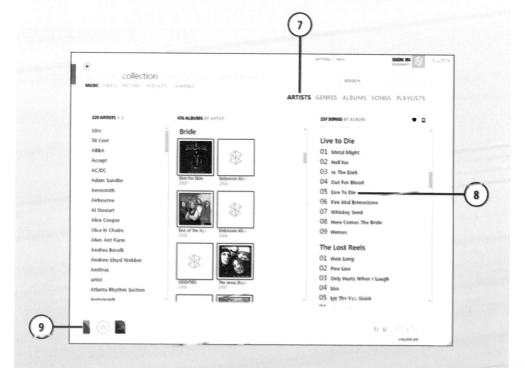

Adding a Playlist to the Phone

To add a playlist to the phone, complete these steps:

1. Connect your phone to the PC.

2. Open the Zune software.

3. Click Collection.

4. Click Music.

5. Click Playlists.

6. Drag the playlist to the phone icon.

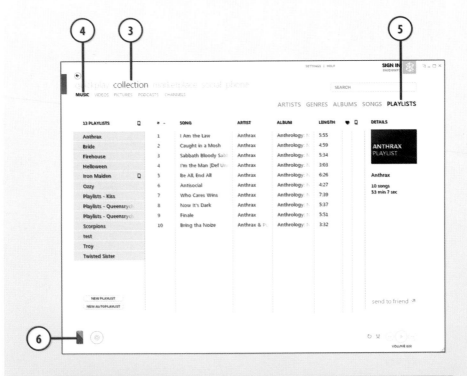

Playlist Content

When you add a playlist to your phone, the songs included in the playlist are automatically synchronized to the phone. There is no need to synchronize each song individually.

Playing a Playlist

To play a playlist, perform the following steps:

1. Press the phone's Start button.

2. Tap Music + Video.

3. Tap Music.

4. Flick the screen to Playlists.

5. Tap the playlist you want to play.

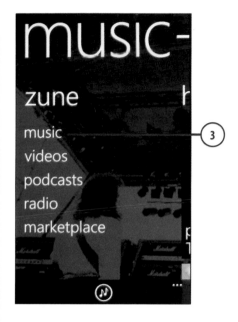

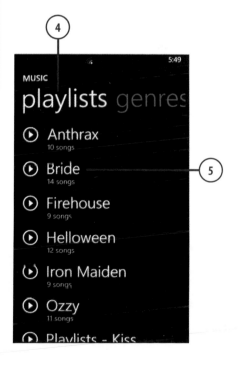

CREDIT WHERE CREDIT IS DUE

In the section on playlists, I created a playlist based on songs from the band Bride (www.bridepub.com). If you enjoy heavy metal music, I recommend checking Bride out because the lead guitarist is none other than Troy Thompson—the technical editor for this book. My personal favorite Bride album is *Snakes in the Playground*.

Creating an Auto Playlist

The Zune software allows you to create a dynamic playlist based on filtering criteria that you specify. When created, an auto playlist can be added to the phone in the same way as an ordinary playlist. You can create an auto playlist by following these steps:

1. Open the Zune software.

2. Click Collection.

3. Click Music.

4. Click Playlists.

5. Click the New Auto Playlist button.

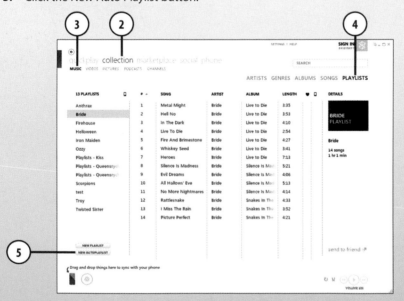

6. Populate the Auto Playlist window with filtering data for the types of music that you would like to include in the playlist.

7. Enter a name for the playlist you are creating.

8. Click OK.

Playing Music in the Background

Windows Phone 7.5 devices are capable of playing music in the background. In other words, if you press the Start button, switch to another app, or even turn off the phone's display, music continues to play. You can control music that is playing in the background by using one of the procedures outlined below:

1. Press the Start button.

2. Tap Music + Video.

3. Flick to the History page.

4. Tap on the track that is currently playing. The resulting screen includes audio controls you can use to pause the audio or to switch tracks.

Audio Controls

The name of the track that is currently playing

Controlling Music From the Start Screen

The other way you can control background audio is to perform these steps:

1. Turn off the phone's display.

2. Turn the display back on.

3. The Start screen contains a set of audio controls that can be used to pause the current track or to switch tracks.

Audio controls and track information on the Windows Phone 7 Start screen

Using the Smart DJ

Windows Phone 7.5 devices include a Smart DJ feature that automatically plays a music mix based on the contents of your collection. The device provides one-touch access to the Smart DJ feature. All you have to do to use it is to go to the Artist screen, tap a favorite artist and then tap the Smart DJ icon. The Smart DJ will play tracks from similar artists.

Tapping the Smart DJ icon causes the phone to play songs from artists that are similar to the one that is currently selected

Sharing Music

Occasionally Smart DJ might play a song that you want to recommend to a friend. If this happens, you can easily send a link to the song by following these steps:

1. From the Smart DJ screen, flick the ... icon upward to reveal the submenu.

2. Tap the Share option.

3. Choose the email account you want to use to share the song.

4. Fill in the recipient information for the message.

5. Tap the Send icon.

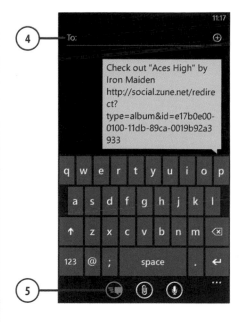

Saving the Mix as a Playlist

If you find that you like the Smart DJ mix, you can save it as a playlist. To do so, follow these steps:

1. From the Album screen, flick the ... icon upward to reveal the submenu.

2. Tap the Save as Playlist option.

3. Enter a name for the new playlist.

It's Not All Good

In preparation for writing this book, I purchased several Windows Phone 7 devices from various vendors. At least one vendor's phone seems to have a bug that prevents this feature from working.

Playing Videos

If you have synchronized videos to your phone, you can play them by performing these steps:

1. Press the Start button.

2. Tap Music + Video.

3. Flick the Music + Video Screen to access the Zune page.

4. Tap Videos.

5. Tap the video you want to play.

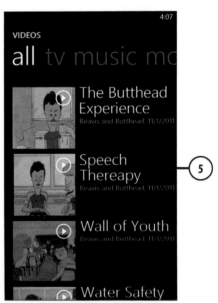

The Video Screen

When you play a video, the video itself is the only thing displayed on the screen. However, if you tap the screen, Windows displays a set of controls, which contains the following:

A. **The name of the video**

B. **Rewind button**

C. **Pause button**

D. **Fast Forward button**

E. **Current video position**

F. **Length of video**

G. **Progress bar**

H. **The Full Screen icon**

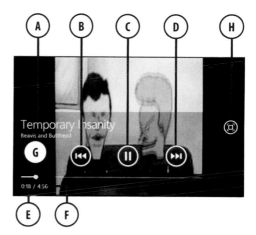

Pause and Play

If you pause a video, the Pause button turns into a Play button that you can press to resume video playback.

Making a Video Selection

When you use the method that was just described to access videos, the phone shows you all of the available videos. However, you can sort the videos by category by flicking the screen to choose a different video category. The available categories include

- **All**—All of the videos on the phone.

- **TV**—Only television shows. TV shows may be grouped into sub containers, with one container for each series (a container for Myth Busters, a container for Beavis and Butthead, and so on).

- **Music**—Music Videos.

- **Movies**—Movies.

- **Personal**—Videos you record yourself.

It's Not All Good

Metadata Nightmares

As you synchronize your videos to the phone, you might discover that all of your videos are lumped into the All container and are not listed in other containers, regardless of the video type. The reason this happens is because Zune looks at a video's metadata to determine which container to place it into. If your collection consists of DVD rips, home movies, YouTube downloads, or video sources that were not specifically intended to be played on the Zune, your videos will likely be missing the metadata that Zune uses to sort the videos into containers. Fortunately, you can add this metadata yourself.

Editing Video Metadata

If you find that your videos are not categorized (or that they are categorized incorrectly), you can modify a video's metadata by completing these steps:

1. Open the Zune software.

2. Click Collection.

3. Click Videos.

4. Right-click the video you need to modify and choose the Edit command from the shortcut menu.

5. When the Edit Video Info dialog box appears, enter the necessary information. You can classify a video by choosing the appropriate setting from the Category drop-down list.

6. Click OK.

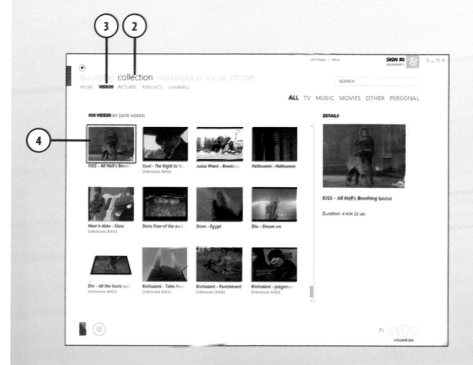

The Edit Video Info screen contains several fields you can edit or populate, which include

A. **Title**—The name of the video.

B. **Category**—The video category (TV, Music, Movies, Personal, Other).

C. **Release Date**—When the video was made.

D. **Genre**—The genre (Action, Comedy, Documentary, and so on).

E. **Description**—A summary of the video.

Populating Fields
The Zune software does not require you to populate any of the available fields. You are free to pick and choose according to your needs.

Additional Fields
Depending on the type of video you are working with, you may be able to edit some additional fields. For example, the video shown in the figure is a music video and hence has an Artist field that is not displayed for other types of videos. Similarly, TV shows have an Episode Title field.

It's Not All Good

Even though the Edit Video Info dialog box contains an option to specify a video's genre, the phone ignores genre information. For example, if your Movies folder contains comedies and action movies, don't expect to see the phone provide you with an Action folder and a Comedy folder. The only type of video the phone groups into folders are TV shows.

Categorizing Television Shows

You can categorize television shows in a way that causes them to be grouped by folder. To do so, follow these steps:

1. Open the Zune software.

2. Click Collection.

3. Click Videos.

4. Right-click the episode you want to categorize and choose the Edit command from the shortcut menu.

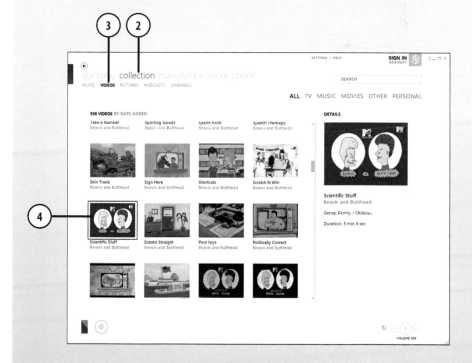

5. When the Edit Video Info dialog box appears, set the Category to Series.

6. Enter a name for the series. The name you enter will be the folder name.

7. Enter a title for the episode.

8. Optionally enter a season number, episode number, release date, genre, and description.

9. Click OK.

BULK EDITING

Go Further

If you have a large video collection, manually editing the video metadata can be a tedious process. Thankfully, it is possible to perform bulk editing of metadata. For example, suppose you have 100 different movies that need to be classified as Movies so that they show up in the Movies folder. Rather than doing each one individually, you can select all of your movies and then right-click them and choose Edit. One word of caution, however, is that any changes that you make apply to every selected video.

Viewing Your Pictures Through the Phone

Just as you can watch videos or listen to music on your phone, you can also browse your collection of photos. Unlike music, videos, and podcasts, however, photos are not accessible through the phone's Music + Videos hub. Instead, you have to access your photos through the Pictures hub. The

Pictures hub is discussed in detail in the next chapter, but for right now I want to show you how to access the pictures you have synced to your phone. To access your photos, perform the following steps:

Viewing Pictures

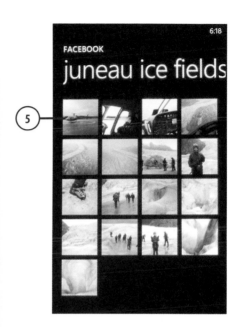

1. Press the Start button.

2. Tap Pictures.

3. When the Pictures Hub opens, tap either Camera Roll (for pictures taken with the phone's camera), Albums (for pictures synchro- nized from the Zune software), Date (to view pictures sorted by date), or People (to see pictures posted by your social networking friends).

4. Depending on which option you have chosen, you might have to tap one or more subfolders.

5. Tap the picture you want to view.

6. You can move from one picture to the next by flicking the screen.

Photo Location

The phone uses the Images folder to store pictures that have been synced from the Zune software. Photos are arranged within the Images folder using the same hierarchy as was used within the Zune software. As such, you might have to tap through multiple folders to access your pictures depending on how your photos were organized on your PC.

Radio

All Windows Phone 7 devices come equipped with a built-in FM radio. You can access the radio through the phone's Music+Videos hub. Additionally, you can compile a list of favorite radio stations that acts as a preset list.

To access the radio interface, go to the Music + Video page, flick to the Zune page if necessary, and Tap Radio.

When you access the Radio interface, several pieces of information are displayed:

A. **Add to Favorites**

B. **Station Identification**

C. **Tuner**

D. **RDS display of station name and song title (if available)**

E. **Favorites List (station presets)**

F. **Play button**

Tuning a Radio Station

To tune a radio station, simply

1. Flick your finger along the list of frequencies until the desired channel is displayed.

2. Tap the Play button to begin playing the selected station.

3. Use the hardware Volume buttons to adjust the radio volume.

Pausing the Radio

When you press Play, the Play button turns into a Pause button that you can use to stop the radio from playing. This is the only way to turn off the radio. If you press the phone's power button, the display turns off, but the radio continues playing until you go back in and press the Pause button. You can access the Pause button either in the Music+Video hub or on the phone's Start screen.

It's Not All Good

Most, If not all, Windows Phone devices use the headphone cord as a radio antenna. As such, you will not be able to listen to the radio unless you are using a set of wired headphones.

It is also worth noting that you can only tune FM stations. Unlike Zune HD, Windows Phone does not support HD radio.

Adding a Radio Station to Your Favorites List

If you have a favorite radio station, you can add that station to a favorites list to make the station easily accessible. To do so, complete these steps:

1. Tune the radio station by flicking your finger across the tuner.

2. Tap the Add to Favorites icon.

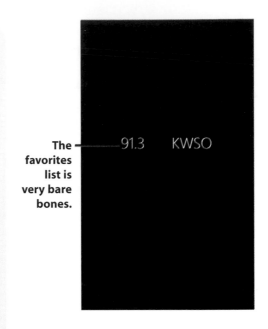

The favorites list is very bare bones.

Confirmation

Windows Phone does not display any sort of message indicating that a radio station has been added to your Favorites list. The only indication that the operation was successful is that the plus sign on the Add to Favorites turns to a minus sign.

Accessing Your Favorite Radio Stations

You can access your favorite radio stations at any time by doing the following:

1. Press the Start button.

2. Tap Music + Videos

3. Flick to the Zune menu if necessary.

4. Tap Radio.

5. Tap the Favorites icon.

6. Tap the listing for the station you want to tune.

Its Not All Good

Removing a Favorite Station

If you need to remove a radio station from your favorites list, you can do so by following these steps:

1. Press the Start button.

2. Tap Music + Videos

3. Flick to the Zune menu if necessary.

4. Tap Radio.

5. Tap the Favorites icon.

6. Tap the station you want to remove.

7. When Zune tunes the station, tap the Remove from Favorites icon.

History

The phone's History screen displays the media you have played most recently. This screen not only displays media that is stored on the phone, but also recent radio stations. You can use the History screen as a quick playlist if you would like to replay something that you have recently listened to.

You can access the History screen by doing the following:

Playing Music from the History Page

1. Press the Start button.

2. Tap Music + Videos

3. Flick the Zune interface until the History screen is displayed. This screen displays the items that were played most recently.

The History screen displays your most recently played media.

Displaying New Content

The Zune interface provides quick access to the media that was added to the phone most recently. You can access the phone's most recently added media by taking the following steps:

1. Press the Start button.

2. Tap Music + Video.

3. Flick the Music + Video Screen to access the Zune page.

4. Flick to New. The New screen displays the most recently added items.

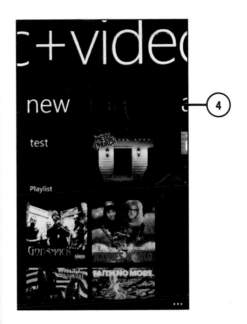

Not So New Content

The New screen continues to display the most recently added content, even after you have played that content. Items remain on the New screen until you add additional media to the phone.

Erasing All Content

Sometimes it is handy to be able to wipe all of the multimedia content from your phone and start over. The easiest way to accomplish this without completely resetting the phone to its factory defaults is to use the Erase All Content option. To do so, follow these steps:

1. Open the Zune software.

2. Plug your phone into your computer.

3. Click Phone.

4. Click Settings.

5. Click Sync Options.

6. Click the Erase All Content button.

7. When prompted, click Yes to erase all of the synced media from the phone.

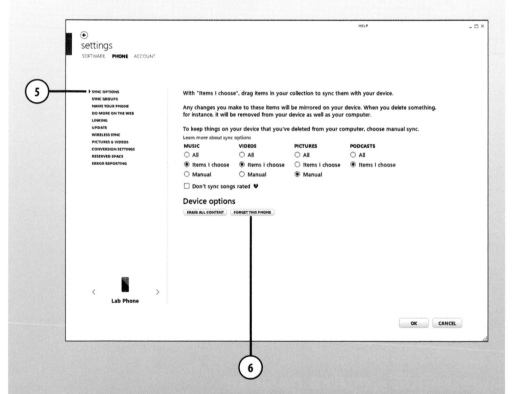

Managing Multiple Devices

Sometimes you might need to manage synchronizations for multiple devices through the Zune software. For example, if you have a Windows Phone device and a Zune HD (or multiple Windows Phone devices), the Zune software is used for managing both devices. In these types of situations, a separate icon is created for each device. You can synchronize media with a specific device by dragging the media to the icon that represents the desired device.

The Zune software can manage multiple Windows Phone and / or Zune devices.

Forgetting a Device

Occasionally it might be necessary to disassociate your phone from the Zune software. You can accomplish this by following these steps:

1. Open the Zune software.

2. Plug your phone into your computer.

3. Click Phone.

4. Click Settings.

5. Click Sync Options.

6. Click Forget This Phone.

7. When prompted, click OK to clear all of the history and settings for the phone.

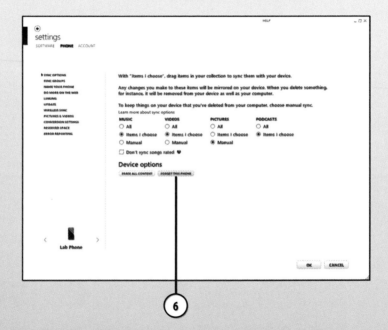

You can take pictures with your phone, or access yours and your friend's photo albums.

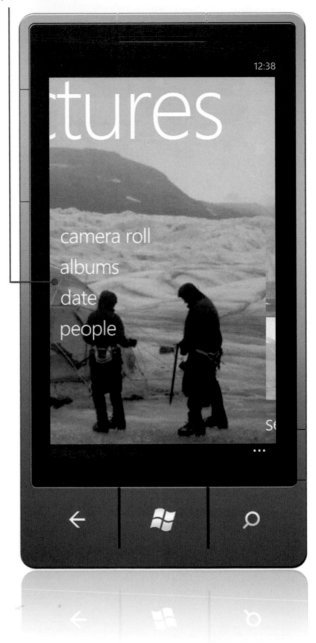

Windows Phone 7 comes with a number of different built-in applications and also gives you the option of downloading additional apps through the Marketplace Hub. In this chapter, you learn about all of the standard built-in apps as well as how to find and install apps from the Marketplace hub. Keep in mind that mobile phone manufacturers and cellular service providers typically add their own proprietary apps to their phones and that such apps are not covered in this chapter, given that they are not technically a part of the Windows Phone.

Windows Phone 7 Apps

Alarms

Windows Phone has a built-in app that allows the phone to act as an alarm clock. This app can be handy for those who travel and forget to bring an alarm clock with them.

Setting an Alarm

You can set an alarm on your phone by completing these steps:

1. Press the Start button.

2. Flick the arrow icon to access the App list.

3. Tap Alarms.

4. Tap the Add icon.

5. Tap the Time field.

6. Set the time for the alarm.

7. Tap the Done icon.

8. Tap the Repeats field.

9. Select the check boxes corresponding to the days when you wish for the alarm to sound.

10. Tap the Done icon.

11. Tap the Sound field.

12. Choose the alarm sound you want to use. You can preview an alarm sound by tapping its Play icon.

13. Tap the Name field.

14. Enter a name for your alarm.

15. Tap the Done icon.

16. Tap the Save icon.

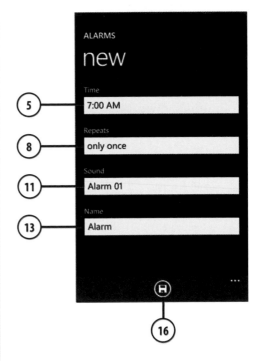

Disabling an Alarm

If you set an alarm and then later decide you do not need the alarm after all, you can easily disable it. To do so, follow these steps:

1. Press the Start button.

2. Flick the arrow icon to access the App List.

3. Tap Alarms.

4. Locate the alarm you want to disable.

5. Set the alarm's slidebar to Off.

Deleting an Alarm

Disabling an alarm simply suspends the alarm so it is not active; it does not delete the alarm. If you want to delete an alarm, you can do so by completing these steps:

1. Press the Start button.

2. Flick the arrow icon to access the App List.

3. Tap Alarms.

4. Tap the alarm that you want to delete.

5. Tap the Delete icon.

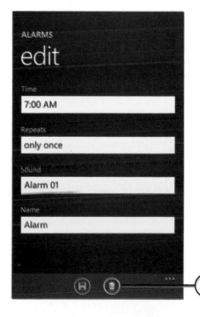

Calculator

A good calculator has become a staple for almost every mobile device, and Windows Phone is no exception. The built-in calculator can be used for simple arithmetic or for scientific calculations.

Accessing the Calculator

You can access the phone's calculator by following these steps:

1. Tap the Start button.

2. Flick the arrow icon to scroll to the App List.

3. Tap Calculator.

Windows Phone 7 offers a basic calculator.

The Scientific Calculator

Although the Calculator app might at first appear to be very basic, Windows Phone does include a scientific calculator. You can access it by opening the Calculator app in the manner just described and then turning the phone sideways. When you do, the Calculator is displayed in Scientific mode.

Turning the phone sideways reveals a scientific calculator.

Calendar

As you would probably expect, the Calendar app is designed to help you keep track of your daily activities. In addition, this app can be used to create and manage meetings in much the same way as you can using Outlook 2010.

Accessing the Calendar

The calendar is accessible directly from the Start screen. You can access the calendar by pressing the Start button and tapping the Calendar tile. The Calendar live tile displays the next appointment on your phone's Start screen.

The calendar is also accessible through the App list by taking the following steps:

1. Press the Start button.

2. Flick the arrow icon to access the App list.

3. Tap Calendar.

Your next appointment is displayed on the Calendar live tile.

Calendar Views

The Calendar opens to Agenda view, unless there are no appointments, in which case it opens to Day view. These views are similar, but the Agenda view only displays your appointments for today, whereas Day view allows you to look at the appointments for the next few days.

Agenda View

Agenda view contains several elements including

A. **View**—You can flick the view to switch between Agenda, To-Do, and Day views.

B. **Today**—Confirmation that this is today's agenda.

C. **Time of the next appointment**.

D. **Name of the appointment**.

E. **The appointment's scheduled duration**.

F. **Your availability**—The availability is color-coded to reflect your appointment status. Availability is discussed later in this chapter.

G. **Today**—This icon displays the current date and when tapped returns you to today on the calendar.

H. **New Icon**—Tap this icon to create an additional appointment.

I. **Month Icon**—Tap this icon to access month view.

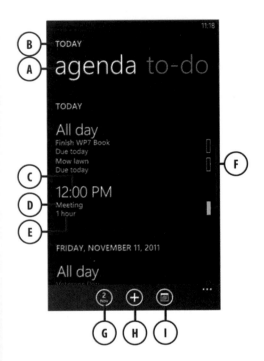

Day View

Day view displays your schedule for today but also allows you to flick the screen up and down to access the appointments for the next few days. This view contains several different elements.

A. **View**—You can flick between Agenda view and Day view.

B. **Time of day**.

C. **Appointment**.

D. **Today**—Tapping this icon causes today's schedule to be displayed.

E. **New Icon**—Used for adding an appointment to the calendar.

F. **Month Icon**—Puts the calendar into Month view.

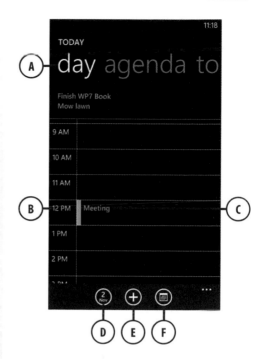

To-Do View

The To-Do view allows you to view your task list (your to-do list). The To-Do view includes several elements including

A. **Current time**

B. **Currently selected view**

C. **Task name**

D. **Task details**

E. **New button**

F. **Select button**

G. **Submenu icon**

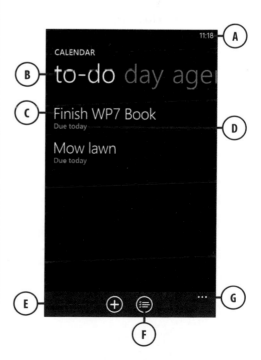

Accessing a Full Month

Even though the Calendar app defaults to displaying the current day's events, you can view appointment information on a monthly calendar as well. To do so, simply go into either Day view or Agenda view and tap the Month View icon. This causes Windows to display a calendar for the current month.

Month view allows you to view an entire month. —

The Small Print

Even though Month view displays your appointments for the month, the text is generally way too small to read. You can access Day or Agenda views for a specific day by going into Month view and then double-tapping the day you want to look at.

Just as you can view the current month, you can access past and future months by tapping the name of the month that is displayed above the calendar. Doing so reveals a screen that lets you choose the month and year you want to view.

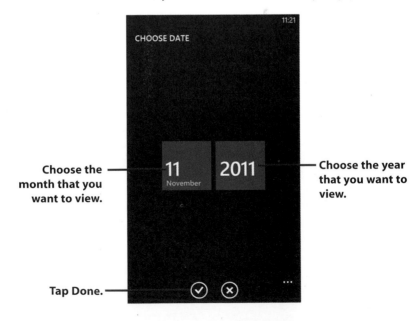

Choose the month that you want to view.

Choose the year that you want to view.

Tap Done.

Viewing a Specific Date

Often times you want to look at the details for a specific date. Switching the date you are viewing from Day view or Agenda view can be impractical if you need to go more than a few days into the future. If you want to look at another date it is easier to tap the Month View icon and then double-tap the date you want to view. After doing so, tap the day you want to view.

Creating an Appointment

You can add an appointment to the calendar from the Day view or the Agenda View screen by tapping the Add Appointment icon. When you do, the New Appointment screen prompts you for several appointment details including

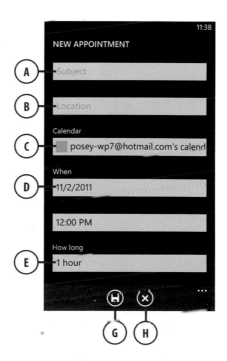

A.   **Subject**—The name of the appointment.

B.   **Location**—Where you need to be for the appointment.

C.   **Calendar**—Allows you to choose which mailbox's calendar the appointment will be added to.

D.   **When**—The When option always picks the current date, but you can tap the date or time fields to pick a different date or time slot.

E.   **How Long**—The anticipated duration of the appointment.

F.   **More Details**—Tap the More Details button if you need to create a meeting or if you need to add additional details to the appointment.

G.   **Save Button**—Save the appointment to your calendar.

H.   **Cancel Button**—Delete the appointment.

Additional Details

When you create a new appointment, you have the option of supplying some additional details that are geared more toward business users. To do so, begin creating a new appointment and then tap the More Details button. The extra details that are available to you include

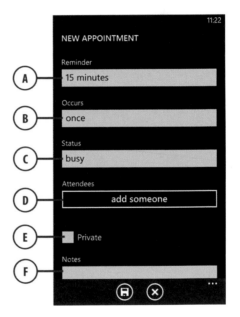

A. **Reminder**—Specify when you want your phone to remind you of an upcoming appointment.

B. **Occurs**—By default, appointments occur only once, but you have the option of setting up a recurring appointment.

C. **Status**—How you want your status to be displayed to those with whom you have shared your calendar.

D. **Attendees**—Allows you to invite someone to a meeting.

E. **Private**—Select this check box to block those with whom you have shared your calendar from viewing the appointment details.

F. **Notes**—You can enter any additional required information about the appointment.

Creating a Recurring Appointment

You can easily create a recurring appointment through your phone. To do so, follow these steps:

1. Press the Start button.

2. Tap the Calendar tile.

3. Tap the New Appointment icon.

4. Enter a subject and a location for the new appointment.

5. Specify the date and time of the first appointment.

6. Enter the appointment duration.

7. Tap More Details.

8. Tap the Occurs field.

9. Tap the recurrence frequency.

10. Tap the Save Button.

It's Not All Good

Even though the phone does allow you to create recurring appointments, the recurrence options are somewhat limited. For example, even though you can set an appointment to recur on the tenth of every month or on every Saturday, there is no way to set a custom recurrence schedule. For example, you can't create a recurring appointment for the second Tuesday of each month.

The Appointment Status

When you create a new appointment, one of the options you can set (after tapping the More Details button) is the appointment's status. When you set an appointment's status, you are actually configuring Outlook free/busy information for the block of time occupied by the appointment.

When you create an appointment, Windows automatically sets the status for the corresponding block of time to Busy. That way, if someone looks at your shared calendar or tries to schedule a meeting with you, he sees you are busy at that particular time. Although Busy is usually an appropriate status, there are four status options that you can choose from:

- **Free**—Even though an appointment is on your calendar, it isn't important and you can be available at that time if necessary.

- **Tentative**—The appointment has not yet been confirmed.

- **Busy**—The appointment is a firm commitment, and you are unavailable during that time slot.

- **Out of the Office**—This option is most appropriate when you are on vacation or when traveling for business.

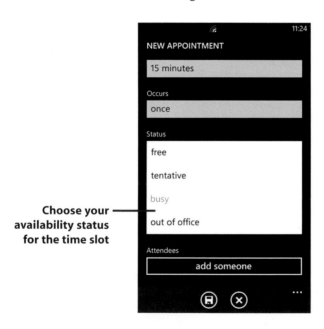

Choose your availability status for the time slot

Calendar Sharing

Even though Windows Phone supports the use of Outlook free/busy information, the phone does not fully support calendar sharing. In other words, you cannot share your calendar through the phone's Calendar app, nor can you open someone else's calendar. Such activities must be performed through Microsoft Office Outlook or through Outlook Web Access/Outlook Web App.

Creating a Meeting

Windows Phone's Calendar app contains native functionality for creating meetings. Although the app doesn't offer all of the options found in a full-blown version of Outlook (such as automatically searching attendee's calendars for a meeting time that is good for everyone), the phone does have the basics covered. If you want to schedule a meeting, follow these steps:

1. Press the Start button.

2. Tap the Calendar tile.

3. Tap the New Appointment icon.

4. Enter a subject and a location for the meeting.

5. Pick a date and time for the meeting.

6. Specify the anticipated meeting duration.

7. Tap the More Details button.

8. Tap the Add Someone button.

9. Tap the Add Someone button that is located in the Required section.

10. Tap the name of the person you want to invite.

11. If there are any additional required attendees, tap the Add Someone icon again and choose the attendees.

12. If you want to invite any optional attendees, tap the Add Someone icon found in the Optional section.

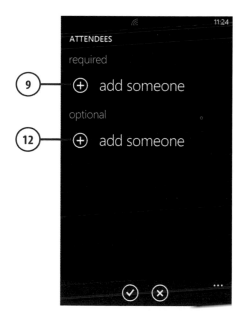

13. Tap the name of the person you want to invite.

14. Tap the Check mark icon.

15. Tap the Save icon.

Meeting Attendees

Windows Phone normally only allows you to send someone a meeting request if you have that person set up as a contact through the People hub. However, some mail providers allow you to search for meeting attendees. For example, if you have Gmail set up on your phone, you can tap the Search button found on the Choose a Contact screen, and you will be allowed to search the Gmail directory.

Responding to a Meeting Invitation

When someone sends you a meeting invitation, that invitation will show up in your inbox just like any other meeting invitation would. When a meeting invitation is viewed through the phone, it looks like any other email message. However, when you tap the Respond button, you are given options to accept, tentatively accept, or decline the invitation.

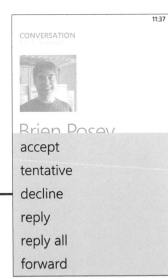

These are your options for responding to an invitation.

If you open the message and then flick the … icon upward, you are given the option of proposing a new time for the meeting.

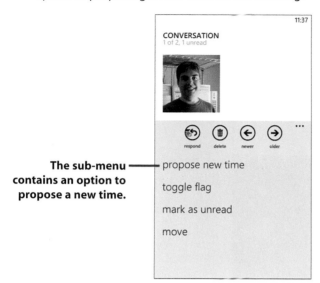

The sub-menu contains an option to propose a new time.

Customizing Your Calendar's Contents

Windows Phone devices can be linked to multiple email accounts, and generally each email account has a corresponding calendar. However, Windows Phone devices do not offer separate calendars for each email account. Instead, the contents of each of your email calendars are aggregated into a unified calendar view. You can, however, control what type of information is displayed on the calendar. To do so, follow these steps:

1. Press the Start button.

2. Tap the Calendar tile.

3. Go to the Day or Agenda view.

4. Flick the … icon upward to reveal the submenu.

5. Tap Settings.

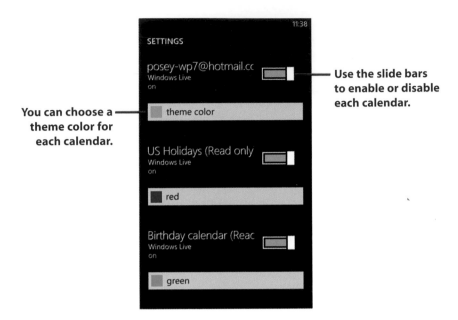

You can choose a theme color for each calendar.

Use the slide bars to enable or disable each calendar.

As you can see in the figure, you have the ability to turn each of your calendars on or off by using a simple slidebar. If you turn a calendar off, its contents do not appear on the Windows Phone calendar.

You are also given the option of picking a color for each of the calendars. Color coding the calendar entries makes it easier to determine which calendar an appointment came from.

The To-Do List

If you choose to synchronize the Task List from your Exchange Server mailbox, the items from the Task List are displayed in the calendar's To-Do view. Of course you are free to use the To-Do view whether you are synchronizing tasks with an Exchange mailbox or not.

Creating a New Task

You can create a new task by following these steps:

1. Press the Start button.

2. Tap the Calendar icon.

3. Switch to To-Do view.

4. Tap the New icon.

5. Enter your task details.

6. Click the Save button.

The New To-Do screen includes several elements including

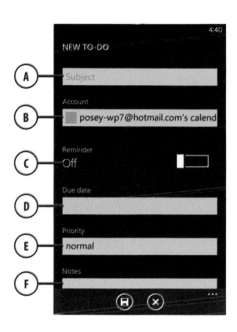

A. **Subject**—This is where you specify the name of the task.

B. **Account**—This is the email account with which the to-do item will be associated.

C. **Reminder**—You can turn the reminder on if you want Windows to alert you when the task is due.

D. **Due Date**—This is when the task needs to be completed.

E. **Priority**—You can set a task's priority to High, Low, or Normal.

F. **Notes**—This is where you enter the details of the task.

Editing a Task

If you need to modify a task, you can do so by following these steps:

1. Press the Start button.

2. Tap the Calendar icon.

3. Switch to To-Do view.

4. Tap the task you want to edit.

5. Tap the Edit button.

6. Make your modifications.

7. Tap the Save button.

Completing a Task

When you have finished a task, Windows expects you to mark the task as completed. This ensures that the task does not continue to appear among the other tasks that must be completed. You can tell Windows that a task has been completed by following these steps:

1. Press the Start button.
2. Tap the Calendar icon.
3. Switch to To-Do view.
4. Tap and hold the task that has been completed.
5. Tap Complete.

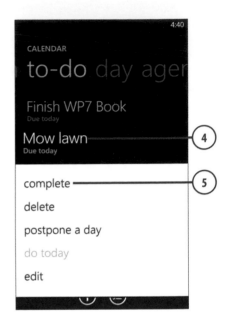

Completing Multiple Tasks

Occasionally you might complete several tasks at once. In this type of situation it is easier to perform a bulk completion rather than flagging each individual task as complete. If you have several tasks completed, you can designate them as complete by following these steps:

1. Press the Start button.
2. Tap the Calendar icon.
3. Switch to To-Do view.
4. Tap the Select button.
5. Select the check boxes for each completed task.
6. Tap the Complete button.

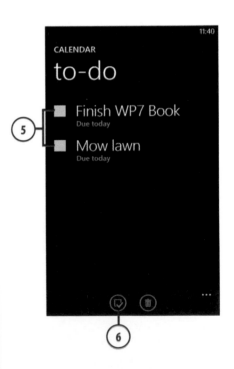

Viewing Completed Tasks

Occasionally you might find you
need to look back at your completed
tasks. You can see your completed
tasks by following these steps:

1. Press the Start button.

2. Tap the Calendar icon.

3. Switch to To-Do view.

4. Flick the … icon upward to reveal
    the submenu.

5. Tap Show Completed.

Activating a Completed Task

If you accidentally flag a task as completed, you can reactivate the task. To
do so, follow these steps:

1. Press the Start button.

2. Tap the Calendar icon.

3. Switch to To-Do view.

4. Flick the … icon upward to reveal
    the submenu.

5. Tap Show Completed.

These—
tasks
have been
completed.

6. Tap and hold the task you want to reactivate (or use the Select icon to select multiple completed tasks).

7. Tap Activate.

Postponing a Task

If you need to postpone a task, you can easily do so by modifying it in the manner previously described and then specifying a new date. However, Windows Phone also provides a shortcut you can use if you want to postpone a task until tomorrow. To move a task to tomorrow, follow these steps:

1. Press the Start button.

2. Tap the Calendar icon.

3. Switch to To-Do view.

4. Tap and hold the task you want to postpone.

5. Tap Postpone a Day.

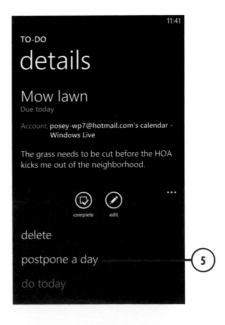

Deleting a Task

If you want to remove a task without completing it, you can delete the task by following these steps:

1. Press the Start button.

2. Tap the Calendar icon.

3. Switch to To-Do view.

4. Tap and hold the task you want to delete.

5. Tap Delete.

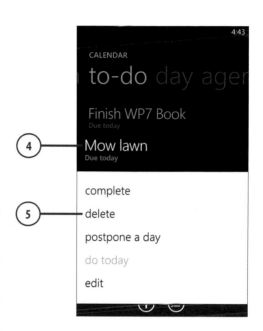

Doing a Task Today

Occasionally you might have a task scheduled for a future date but decide it needs to be done today. When this occurs, you can use a shortcut to change the task's date to today. To do so, follow these steps:

1. Press the Start button.

2. Tap the Calendar icon.

3. Switch to To-Do view.

4. Tap and hold the task you want to do today.

5. Tap Do Today.

Viewing Tasks By Priority

As previously mentioned, Windows Phone allows you to prioritize your tasks. That being the case, it is possible to sort the list of upcoming tasks by priority. To do so, follow these steps:

1. Press the Start button.

2. Tap the Calendar icon.

3. Switch to To-Do view.

4. Flick the ... icon upward to reveal the submenu.

5. Tap Sort by Priority.

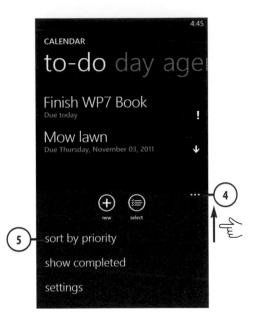

Camera

Every Windows Phone device is equipped with a five megapixel camera that can also be used as a video camera. The pictures and video you record with the built-in camera can be stored in the device, synchronized to your Zune collection, or shared with others.

Taking a Picture

To take a still photo using a Windows Phone device, follow these steps:

1. Press the Camera button on the side of the device.

2. Aim the device at the subject you want to photograph.

3. Press the Camera button half way down to focus the camera.

4. Press the Camera button again to snap the picture.

Geo Tagging

Windows Phone 7.5 devices contain a geo tagging feature that appends your GPS location to your photos. When you use the camera for the first time, you might receive a prompt asking you if you want to allow location data to be used.

Adjusting the Zoom

Although most Windows Phone 7 devices do not have a true zoom lens, the devices do offer a limited digital zoom. You can zoom the camera in on a subject by completing these steps:

1. Press the Camera button.

2. Aim the camera at the subject you want to photograph.

3. Use the + and – icons to zoom in or out.

4. Press the camera button half way down to focus the picture.

5. Press the Camera button again to snap the picture.

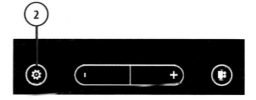

Zoom Out   Zoom In

Photo Settings

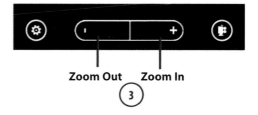

There are a number of different camera settings you can adjust prior to snapping a picture. These settings affect things like the picture's coloring and resolution. You can adjust the photo settings by following these steps:

1. Press the Camera button.

2. Tap the Settings icon.

The available settings vary widely from one device to another. Each manufacturer integrates settings specific to their camera.

The available settings vary from phone to phone.

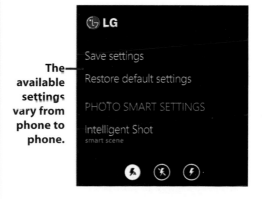

Enabling the Camera's Flash

Windows Phone cameras are equipped with a flash. You can enable the flash by following these steps:

1. Press the Camera button.

2. Tap the Settings icon.

3. Tap the Flash or the Automatic Flash icon.

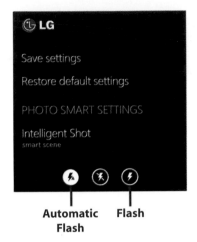

Automatic Flash   **Flash**

Disabling the Camera's Flash

Occasionally you might need to disable the camera's flash prior to taking a picture. You can disable the flash by completing these steps:

1. Press the Camera button.

2. Tap the Settings icon.

3. Tap the Disable Flash icon.

Video Mode

Although the phone's camera is configured by default to take still pictures, it
can also be used to film video. This
video can then be synchronized to your
Zune collection or shared with others.

Switching Between Photo
and Video

You can switch the camera into video
mode by following these steps:

1. Press the Camera button.

2. Tap the Video icon.

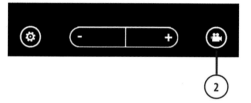

Recording a Video

Recording a video is as simple as snapping a still photo. To do so, complete
these steps:

1. Press the Camera button.

2. Ensure that the device is in video
   mode.

3. Aim the camera.

4. Press the Camera button to begin
   recording. A counter appears on
   the screen to let you know how
   long you have been recording.

5. Press the Camera button to stop
   recording.

Watching Recorded Videos
After you record a video, you can watch it through the Zune interface, which was discussed in the previous chapter.

Adjust Video Settings

Just as you can configure various settings for the still camera, you can also
adjust various video settings such as
the video resolution and the focus
mode. Once again, the actual settings
available are device-specific and vary
from one model of phone to the
next. To access the video settings, follow these steps:

1. Press the Camera button.

2. Ensure that the device is in video
   Mode.

3. Tap the Settings icon.

Adjusting the Video Resolution

Before you record a video, it is
worth checking to make sure your
phone is set to use the optimal
video resolution. Some phones
default to using VGA resolution
(640 x 480) even though the camera supports Hi-Def video at 720P
(1280 x 720). Of course lower
video resolutions consume less
storage space, so that is something to consider if your phone is
short on storage.

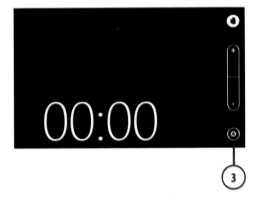

00:00

Using the Video Light

If you need a little bit of extra light for your video, you will be happy to know that the camera's flash can double as a video light. To enable the video light, follow these steps:

1. Press the Camera button.

2. Ensure that the device is in video mode

3. Tap the Settings icon

4. Tap the Video Light icon.

5. Press the Back button.

Malfunctioning Video Light

If the video light does not come on, it doesn't necessarily mean you are doing something wrong. Some phones are designed to override the video light setting if sufficient lighting is available.

Turning Off the Video Light

The video light can be turned off in a similar manner to the way that it is turned on. To disable the video light, follow these steps:

1. Press the Camera button.

2. Ensure that the device is in video mode.

3. Tap the Settings icon.

4. Tap the icon to turn off the video light.

5. Press the Back button.

Viewing Your Pictures

You can view the pictures you have taken by following these steps:

1. Press the Start button.

2. Tap the Pictures tile.

3. Tap either Camera Roll or Albums.

4. Tap the picture you want to view.

5. You can view other pictures by flicking the screen left and right.

Adding a Picture to Your Favorites

Windows Phone allows you to flag your favorite photos so they can all be viewed together in the Favorites folder. To add a picture to your favorites, follow these steps:

1. Press the Start button.

2. Tap the Pictures tile.

3. Tap either Camera Roll or Albums.

4. Tap the picture you want to add to your favorites.

5. Flick the ... icon upward.

6. Tap Add to Favorites.

Viewing Your Favorite Pictures

You can view your favorite pictures at any time by following these steps:

1. Press the Start button.

2. Tap the Pictures tile.

3. Tap Albums.

4. Flick the screen to access Favorites view.

5. Tap the picture you want to view.

6. You can view other pictures by flicking the screen left and right.

Sorting Pictures by Date

Windows Phone gives you the option of viewing your pictures based on the date when they were taken. To see your pictures grouped by date, follow these steps:

1. Press the Start button.

2. Tap the Pictures tile.

3. Tap Date.

4. Tap the picture you want to view.

5. You can view other pictures by flicking the screen left and right.

Deleting a Picture

Not every picture you snap is going to be something you want to keep forever. You can delete a picture by completing these steps:

1. Tap the Pictures tile.

2. Tap All.

3. Tap Camera Roll.

4. Tap the picture that you want to delete.

5. Flick the ... icon upward.

6. Tap Delete.

7. When Windows asks you if you want to delete the picture, tap Delete.

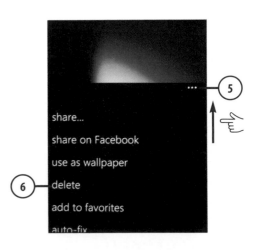

Putting Pictures on Your SkyDrive

Windows Live accounts include free access to SkyDrive. SkyDrive is a 25GB pool of cloud storage you can use to store files and documents. As you can see in the following figure, SkyDrive is directly accessible through the Windows Live Web interface.

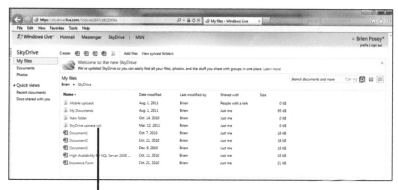

SkyDrive is accessible through Windows Live.

Uploading a Picture to SkyDrive

Windows Phone has the ability to upload pictures from the phone directly to SkyDrive (assuming that the phone has been provisioned with a Windows Live account as discussed in Chapter 3, "Messaging"). To upload photos to SkyDrive, follow these steps:

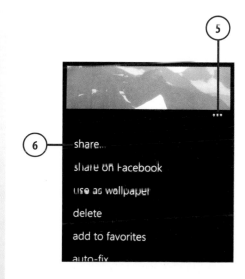

1. Tap the Pictures tile.

2. Tap All.

3. Tap Camera Roll.

4. Tap the picture that you want to upload to SkyDrive.

5. Flick the ... icon upward.

6. Tap Share.

7. Tap SkyDrive

Sharing Your Pictures

After you snap a photo, you can immediately share the picture with your friends by sending them the picture through email or through a text message. Although you can manually compose a new message and attach the picture, you don't have to. You can send the picture directly through the Camera app. To do so, follow these steps:

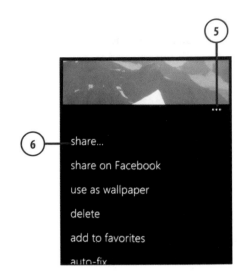

1. Tap the Pictures tile.

2. Tap All.

3. Tap Camera Roll.

4. Tap the picture you want to share.

5. Flick the … icon upward.

6. Tap Share.

7. Tap the email account you want to use to send the picture or pick the Messaging option to send the picture as a text.

8. When the message composition screen opens, enter the email address for the intended recipient.

9. Enter a subject line and/or any desired text.

10. Tap the Send icon.

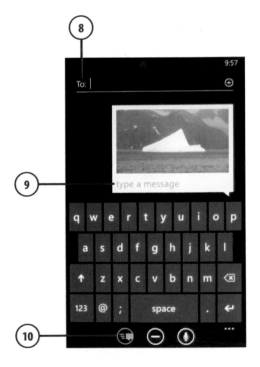

Configuring the Camera's Configuration Settings

In addition to the manufacturer specific camera settings that were discussed earlier, there are also some global configuration options for the camera. You can access these configuration options by following these steps:

1. Press the Start button.

2. Flick the arrow icon to access the App List.

3. Scroll to the bottom of the App List and tap Settings.

4. Flick the screen to the left to access the Application Settings page.

5. Tap Pictures + Camera.

The Pictures + Camera screen contains the following options:

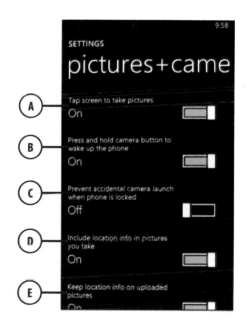

A. **Tap Screen to Tape Pictures—**Allows you to snap a picture without pressing the shutter button.

B. **Press and Hold Camera Button to Wake Up the Phone**—This option allows you to take a picture quickly without having to first power up the phone.

C. **Prevent Accidental Camera Launch When Phone Is Locked**—Prevents you from snapping pictures by accident.

D. **Include Location Info in Pictures You Take** —This option is disabled by default but can be enabled to support geo tagging your photos.

E. **Keep Location Info on Uploaded Pictures**—Controls whether or not location information should be stripped from uploaded pictures.

F. **Automatically Upload to SkyDrive**—If this setting is enabled, every photo you take is sent to SkyDrive. It's a good way to backup your photos as soon as you take them but can be annoying if you take a lot of unimportant pictures you don't plan on keeping.

G.   Keep Location Info on Uploaded Pictures—If you disable this setting, then any geo tagging information is stripped from a photo before it is uploaded to SkyDrive.

H.   Quick Upload Account—The Quick Upload Account option tells you where photos will be uploaded, but the setting that is displayed cannot be changed.

Internet Explorer

Perhaps none of Windows Phone 7's features have been improved over the previous version of Windows Mobile more than Internet Explorer. Previous mobile editions of Internet Explorer could be difficult to use, and many times Web pages did not display properly. Windows Phone 7.5 includes a version of Internet Explorer 9 that is similar to the desktop version and renders most Web pages in exactly the same way that a desktop computer would.

Browsing the Web

Browsing the Web on a Windows Phone device is just as simple as doing so from a computer. To visit a Web page, follow these steps:

1.   Press the Start button.

2.   Tap Internet Explorer.

3.   When the browser opens, enter the URL for the website you want to visit.

The main browser screen includes several elements including:

A.   The address bar

B.   The Refresh icon

C.   The submenu icon

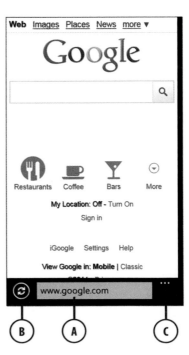

Zooming a Page

Because Windows Phone devices have a much smaller screen than a typical computer, it can be difficult to read the text on a Web page. One way to improve a page's readability is to turn the phone sideways. Upon doing so, the browser rotates so the page is displayed in landscape format.

It is possible to zoom way in on a web page.

Sometimes, even viewing a page in landscape mode isn't enough to make the page readable. In such cases, you can zoom in on the page by using the pinching gesture. After doing so, you can flick the screen in any direction to view the rest of the page.

Adding a Page to Your Favorites

Just as desktop versions of Internet Explorer allow you to maintain a list of favorite web pages, so too does Internet Explorer Mobile. You can add a web page to your list of favorites by following these steps:

1. Press the Start Button.

2. Tap Internet Explorer.

3. Enter the URL for the Web page you want to add to your favorites list.

4. Flick the ... icon upward to reveal the submenu.

5. Tap Add to Favorites.

6. When prompted, verify the name of the page and its URL and make any necessary corrections.

7. Tap the Done icon.

Accessing Your Favorites List

You can access your favorite web pages at any time by following these steps:

1. Press the Start button.

2. Tap the Internet Explorer tile.

3. Flick the ... icon upward to reveal the submenu.

4. Tap Favorites.

5. Tap the page you want to visit.

Removing a Page from Your Favorites

If you accidentally add a page to your favorites list, you can easily remove it from the list by following these steps:

1. Press the Start button.

2. Tap the Internet Explorer tile.

3. Flick the ... icon upward to reveal the submenu.

4. Tap Favorites.

5. Tap and hold the item you want to remove.

6. Tap Delete.

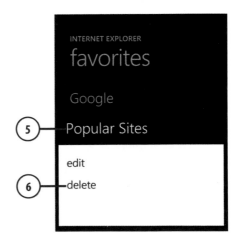

Editing Your Favorites

When you tap and hold an item on your Favorites list, the submenu displays an option to delete the item, but it also offers to let you edit the item. You can use the Edit option to change the name of the page, the URL, or both.

Accessing Your Browsing History

Just as desktop versions of Internet Explorer keep track of the sites you visit, so too does Internet Explorer Mobile. You can use your browsing history list as a handy mechanism for revisiting recently visited websites. You can access the browsing history by completing these steps:

1. Press the Start button.

2. Tap the Internet Explorer tile.

3. Flick the ... icon upward to reveal the submenu.

4. Tap Recent.

Tabbed Browsing

Most of the newer browsers for desktop computers offer a tabbed browsing feature, which lets you open multiple web pages and go back and forth between them. The mobile version of Internet Explorer 9 includes this functionality as well. To see how tabbed browsing works, complete these steps:

1. Press the Start button.

2. Tap the Internet Explorer tile.

3. Flick the ... icon upward to reveal the submenu.

4. Tap Tabs.

5. Tap the New icon to open a new tab.

You can access any of the open tabs at any time by flicking the ... icon to reveal the submenu, tapping Tabs, and then tapping the tab you want to view.

Multitasking

Tabbed browser sessions remain open even after you press the Start button to move on to something else.

Sharing a Web Page

You can share a web page with a friend by emailing or texting her the name of the page and the URL. To send a Web page to someone, follow these steps:

1. Press the Start button.

2. Tap the Internet Explorer tile.

3. Navigate to the web page you want to share.

4. Flick the ... icon upward to reveal the submenu.

5. Tap Share Page.

6. Choose the Messaging option to send the Web page by text or pick the email account you want to use to send the page.

7. Specify who you want to send the page to.

8. Tap Send.

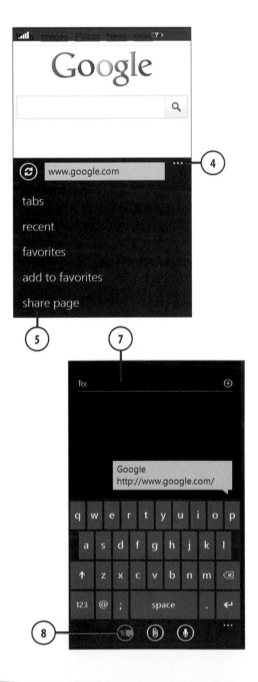

Adding a Page to the Start Screen

If you use a particular web page often, you might want to pin the page to your start screen rather than merely adding it to your favorites. To do so, follow these steps:

1. Press the Start button.

2. Tap the Internet Explorer tile.

3. Navigate to the page that you want to add to the Start menu.

4. Flick the ... icon upward to reveal the submenu.

5. Tap Pin to Start.

Pin to Start Option Unavailable

You will not be able to use the Pin to Start option until the web page has finished loading. Until then the option will be grayed out.

Internet Explorer Settings

There are several different settings that you can manage for Internet Explorer including those related to cookies, suggested sites, and website preferences. You can access the Internet Explorer Settings by following these steps:

1. Press the Start button.

2. Flick the arrow icon to access the App list.

3. Scroll to the bottom of the App list and tap Settings.

4. Flick the Settings screen to the left to access the Application Settings page.

5. Tap Internet Explorer.

The Settings page provides the following options:

A. **Allow Access to My Location**—Allows web pages (such as Bing) to use GPS data.

B. **Allow Cookies on My Phone**—Cookies are allowed by default.

C. **Get Suggestions from Bing as I Type**— This option displays popular URLs as you enter the URL for the page you want to visit.

D. **Allow Internet Explorer to Collect My Browsing History**—This option lets the phone compile a list of websites you have visited.

E. **Website Preference**—By default the phone displays the mobile version of a website if a mobile version exists, but you can choose to always display the desktop version instead.

F. **Open Links From Other Apps In**—This option allows you to control whether links are opened on the current tab or on a new tab.

G. **Delete History**—The Delete History option deletes temporary files, history, cookies, and saved passwords from Internet Explorer.

Clearing Your Browsing History

Internet Explorer Mobile allows you to clear your browser history whenever necessary. Clearing your history removes temporary files, the browsing history, cookies, and any saved passwords. You can clear the browser's history by following these steps:

1. Press the Start button.

2. Tap the Internet Explorer tile.

3. Flick the ... icon upward to reveal the submenu.

4. Tap Settings.

5. Tap Delete History.

6. Tap Delete.

Marketplace

The Marketplace Hub is an online portal through which you can download apps and music for your phone. Many of the apps (and a few of the songs) are free, but most require paying a fee.

The Marketplace Interface

You can access the Marketplace by pressing the Start button and tapping the Marketplace tile. When the Market Place opens, you see a screen that lists the types of items that you can find in the marketplace (Apps, Games, Music, and so on).

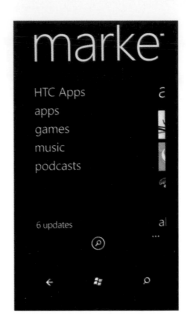

The Marketplace consists of five screens including:

- **Apps**—The Apps screen lets you browse the apps that are available.

- **Games**—The Games screen is like the Apps screen but focuses solely on games.

- **Music**—You can use the Music screen to browse and download music.

- **Featured**—The "Featured" screen doesn't really have a name. It is used to display whatever games, apps, or music are being promoted at the moment.

- **Categories**—Like the Featured screen, the "Categories" screen doesn't really have an official name either. It is designed to let you browse marketplace content by category.

Application Updates

If an update is available for any of your apps, then a number will appear on the Marketplace tile. This number indicates the number of updates that are available.

The number of available updates appears on the Marketplace tile.

If updates are available, you can access them through the Categories screen. The bottom of this screen provides a link to any updates that are available for apps that you have already downloaded. To apply updates, follow these steps:

Updating an Application

1. Press the Start button.

2. Tap the Marketplace tile.

3. Go to the Categories screen.

4. Tap the update notification.

5. Tap the app you want to update or tap the Update All button.

Finding New Applications

Windows Phone makes it easy to search for new apps. To do so, follow these steps:

1. Press the Start button.

2. Tap the Marketplace tile.

3. Go to the Categories screen.

4. Tap Apps.

5. Flick to the Categories screen.

6. Tap the type of app you are interested in (Games, Entertainment, Photo, Lifestyle, and so on).

7. Browse through the list of applications until you find the one you are interested in.

As an alternative, you can search for an application. To do so, follow these steps:

1. Press the Start button.

2. Tap the Marketplace tile.

3. Press the Search button.

4. Enter your search criteria.

5. Browse the search results for an application that meets your needs.

Viewing an Application

When you find an app you would like to install, tap the icon for the app. Windows displays a screen with detailed information about the app. Items on this screen include

A. **Name of App**—You can see the name of the application and the name of the publisher.

B. **App's Icon**—This is the icon that appears in the App list if you choose to install the app.

C. **Price**—Some apps are free, and some are not.

D. **App Rating**—This is a star rating based on feedback from other users.

E. **Description of App**—The description typically outlines the app's features and capabilities.

F. **Show Details**—Most app descriptions include a Show Details button that reveals more detailed information about the app.

G. **The Try Button**—Tap the Try button to install a free trial version of the app.

H. **The Buy Button**—Tap the Buy button to purchase the app.

User Reviews

You can flick the screen to the right to view the app's user reviews.

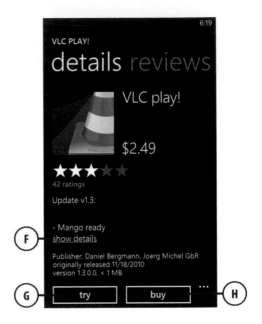

Installing an Application

When you have found an application you want to install, you can install it by completing these steps:

1. Tap the app's icon to reveal its details screen.

2. Tap Try.

3. Some apps might display a screen asking you if you want to allow the app to access device functions such as location information. If such a screen is displayed, tap Allow.

4. The app installs automatically.

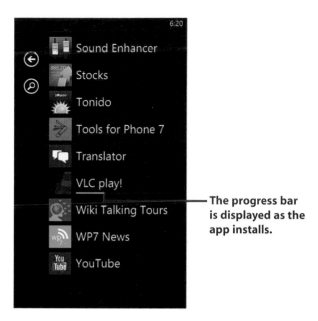

The progress bar is displayed as the app installs.

It's Not All Good

Although apps can be installed directly through the phone in the manner described above, using this method isn't always the best idea. If your phone ever has to be reset to the factory defaults, any apps will be removed from the phone. You can re-download your apps from the Marketplace, but you will have to re-purchase any paid apps. To avoid the risk of having to re-purchase apps that you have already paid for, Microsoft recommends that you install apps through the Zune software rather than directly through your phone. The procedure for doing so is discussed in the next section.

Installing an App Through the Zune Software

Just as you can download and install apps directly through the phone, you can also do so through the Zune software. To do so, follow these steps:

1. Connect your phone to your computer. The Zune software should launch automatically.

2. Click the Marketplace tab.

3. Click Apps.

4. Locate and then click the app you want to download.

5. Click either the Buy button or the Free Trial button for a paid app. If the app is free, click the Free button.

6. If prompted, sign into Windows Live.

7. Click Install.

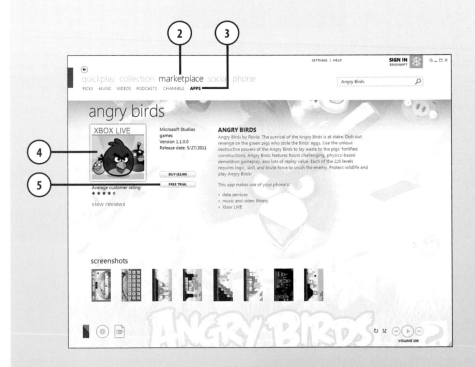

Removing an App

If you would like to remove an app that you have installed, you can do so by following these steps:

1. Press the Start button.

2. Flick the arrow icon to reveal the App list.

3. Tap and hold the app you want to remove.

4. Tap Uninstall.

5. Tap Yes.

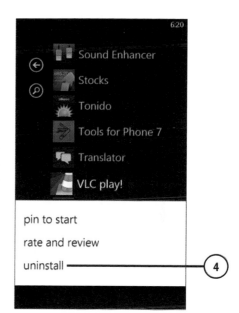

The Zune Marketplace

Although the Marketplace focuses heavily on apps, you can also use it to purchase and download music through an area known as the Zune Marketplace. You can access the Zune Marketplace by completing these steps:

1. Press the Start button.

2. Tap the Marketplace tile.

3. Tap Music. This takes you to the Zune Marketplace.

The Zune Marketplace contains several screens you can flick between. These screens include

- **Artist of the Week**—The latest from a Zune featured artist

- **Featured**—A collection of featured albums from a variety of genres

- **New Releases**—New albums from a variety of Genres

- **Top Albums**—The current top selling albums

- **Genres**—Specific genres you can browse

The Zune marketplace opens to a page displaying the artist of the week.

Browsing by Genre

Unless you have very diverse musical tastes, you will probably be happier if you browse the Zune Marketplace by music genre. That way you can filter the browsing results based on your musical tastes. To browse by music Genre, follow these steps:

1. Press the Start button.

2. Tap the Marketplace tile.

3. Tap Music.

4. Flick the screen to the right until you reach the Genre page.

5. Tap your genre of choice.

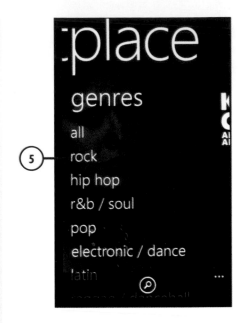

When you pick a genre, Windows Phone 7 displays a list of new releases that fall into that genre.

It's Not All Good

Although Windows Phone gives you many different music genres to choose from, not all genres are represented. For example, heavy metal, bluegrass, and opera are all missing from the list.

When you choose a music genre, you are taken to a page that allows you to browse the available music by several categories including

- New Releases

- Top Songs

- Top Albums

- Top Playlists

- Top Artists

Searching the Zune Marketplace

If you have a specific song or album that you want to purchase from the Market-place, it is easier to search for what you are looking for than to browse through an entire musical genre. To search for an artist, song, album, or playlist, follow these steps:

1. Press the Start button.

2. Tap the Marketplace tile.

3. Tap Music.

4. Tap the Search icon.

5. Enter your search criteria.

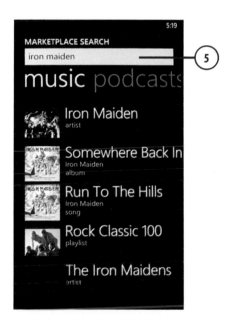

Music Search Results

The search results contain a mixture of albums, artists, songs, and playlists. It is worth noting that this particular search only searches the Zune Marketplace, not your personal music collection. Searching your music collection is discussed in the last chapter of the book.

You can create and edit Microsoft Office directly through your phone!

In this chapter you learn how to work with the mobile versions of Microsoft Word, Excel, PowerPoint, and One Note using your Windows Phone 7.

6

Microsoft Office Mobile

From the very beginning, Microsoft has included mobile versions of the Microsoft Office applications on their mobile operating systems. This tradition has been continued in Windows Phone 7, which offers mobile versions of Microsoft Word, Excel, PowerPoint, and OneNote. The phone is also designed to interact with SharePoint 2010 workspaces.

In previous editions of Windows Mobile, the Microsoft Office apps were usually just enough to get by on. For example, it was possible to receive a Microsoft Word document by email, open it, make a few changes, and send it back. However, many important features were missing. For instance, if a document contained comments, those comments could not be displayed.

The other thing that plagued previous editions of Microsoft Office Mobile was that the applications could be difficult to use on a device with a small screen. Many Windows Mobile 6.1 devices for example required the use of a stylus. Imagine trying to compose a Word document by using a stylus to tap tiny characters on an onscreen keyboard.

With the release of Windows Phone 7, Microsoft has completely redesigned Microsoft Office Mobile. Although none of the Microsoft Office Mobile apps are as full featured as their Office 2010 counterparts, Microsoft has added a great deal of functionality and designed each app's interface so that it can easily be used from a Windows Phone 7 touch screen.

Accessing Microsoft Office

You can get to the Microsoft Office hub by following these steps:

1. Press the Start button.

2. Flick the arrow icon to access the App list screen.

3. Tap Office.

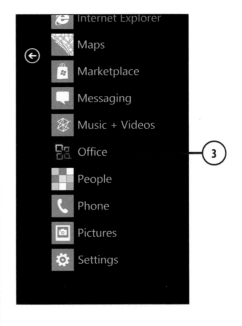

Making Office Accessible from the Start Screen

If you use Microsoft Office often, you can pin it to the Start screen to make it more readily accessible. To do so, follow these steps:

1. Press the Start button.

2. Flick the arrow icon to access the App list screen.

3. Tap and hold the Office icon.

4. Tap Pin to Start.

5. The Office icon is added to the Start screen.

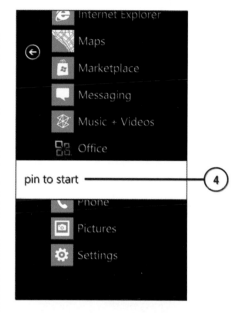

The Microsoft Office Screens

When you initially open Microsoft Office, the Notes screen is displayed. Notes is just one of the screens that is accessible by flicking left and right. The screens that are available within the Microsoft Office hub include

- **Notes**—This screen allows you to create or view One Note documents.

- **Documents**—This screen provides access to all of the Office documents that are stored on the phone.

- **Locations**—The Locations screen allows access to Office documents saved in various locations.

One Note

Microsoft One Note is an application designed to allow you to keep track of multiple notes in a single place. A single One Note document can contain a combination of text, images, and audio notes. Some common uses for One Note documents include shopping lists, meeting notes, invention ideas (with diagrams), and to-do lists.

The Notes screen includes several elements including

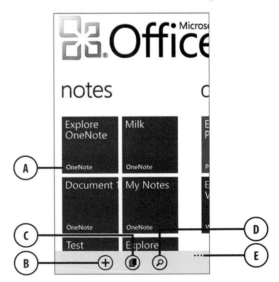

A.   **One Note documents**.

B.   **New**—Tap this icon to create a new One Note document.

C.   **Notebooks**—You can tap the Notebooks icon to view your existing notebooks.

D.   **Search**— Allows you to search for existing One Note documents.

E.   **The Submenu icon**—Flick this icon to access the submenu.

Creating a New One Note Document

You can create a new One Note document by completing these steps:

1. Press the Start button.

2. Flick the arrow icon to access the App list screen.

3. Tap Office.

4. Flick the screen to the Notes page if necessary.

5. Tap New icon.

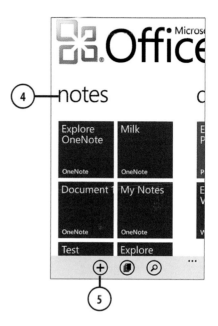

Giving Your One Note Document a Title

When you create a new One Note document, you are prompted to enter a title for the new document, as shown in the next figure.

To assign a title to the document, follow these steps:

1. Tap Enter Title.

2. Enter a name for the document.

3. Tap the document body.

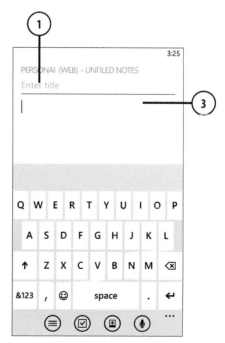

Opening One Note Documents

As you create One Note documents, your most recent documents are displayed directly on the One Note screen. For example, in the next figure, Document 1 is a recently created One Note document.

You can open a One Note document simply by tapping it. Keep in mind, however, that the One Note screen only lists the most recently created documents. If you need to open an older document, you can do so by following these steps:

1. Navigate to the One Note screen.

2. Tap the Search button.

3. Enter your search query.

4. Tap the document you want to open.

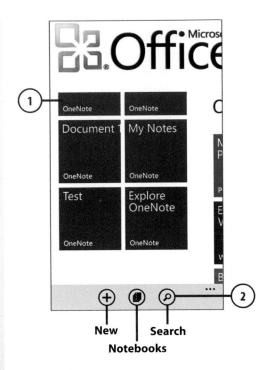

New   Search
Notebooks

Deleting a One Note Document

As you begin to accumulate One Note documents on your phone, you might eventually decide to free up some space by getting rid of some older documents. To delete a One Note document, complete these steps:

1. Navigate to the One Note page.

2. Tap the Search icon and locate the document that you want to delete.

3. Tap and hold the document.

4. Tap Delete.

5. You see a message indicating that the document will be permanently deleted. Tap Yes to delete the document.

Limited Delete Options

You can only delete a One Note document by tapping the Search button and then searching for the document you want to delete. You cannot delete a document by tapping and holding the listing for the document on the main One Note screen.

Pinning a Document to the Start Screen

As is the case with other types of documents, One Note documents can be pinned to the Start screen. To do so, follow these steps:

1. Navigate to the One Note page.

2. Tap and hold the document you want to pin to the Start screen. If the document is unlisted, tap the Search icon and then locate, tap, and hold the document you want to pin to the Start screen.

3. Tap Pin to Start.

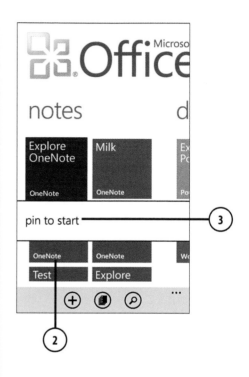

Creating a Numbered List

You can easily create a numbered list in One Note by following these steps:

1. Create a new document or open an existing document.

2. Tap the document body.

3. Flick the … icon upward to reveal the submenu.

4. Tap Numbered List.

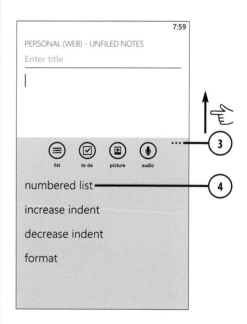

5. The number 1 will automatically be added to the document. Type your first list item next to 1.

6. Press Enter and type the next list item.

7. When you get to the end of your list, press Enter twice to end the numbering.

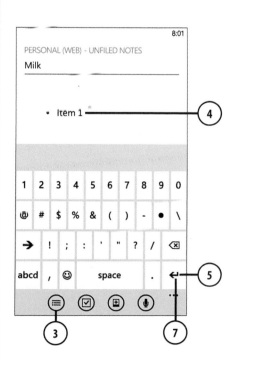

This is a numbered list.

Creating a Bullet List

Creating a bulleted list works very similarly to creating a numbered list. To create a bulleted list, follow these steps:

1. Create a new One Note document or open an existing document.

2. Tap in the document body.

3. Tap the List icon.

4. Type your first item next to the bullet that Windows adds to the screen.

5. Press Enter.

6. Add any additional list items, pressing Enter after each.

7. At the end of the list, press Enter twice.

Adding Pictures

One of the things that makes One Note so unique is that it allows you to combine various types of media into a single document. You can add pictures to your One Note document by following these steps:

1. Create a new One Note document or open an existing document.

2. Tap in the document body.

3. Tap the Picture icon.

4. Tap the picture that you want to add to the document.

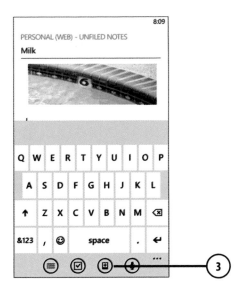

Adding Pictures

It is worth noting that you can only add a picture that is stored on your phone (or you can add a picture from the phone's camera). You cannot add images from the Internet without first using the Zune software to add the image to your collection.

Adding Audio

One Note also accepts audio notes. To add an audio note to your One Note document, follow these steps:

1. Create a new One Note document or open an existing document.

2. Tap in the document body.

3. Tap the Audio icon.

4. Record your note.

5. Tap Stop. The audio note is inserted into the document.

Playing an Audio Note

You can play an audio note at any time simply by tapping it.

It's Not All Good

Even though the desktop version of One Note allows you to add prerecorded audio files to your documents, the mobile version does not support doing so. You can only add audio that you record on the spot.

Adding a To-Do List

Just as you can add pictures and audio notes to a One Note document, you can also add a To-Do list. To do so, follow these steps:

1. Create a new One Note document or open an existing document.

2. Tap in the document body.

3. Tap the To Do icon.

4. One Note automatically creates a check box. Enter a To-Do item next to the check box.

5. Press Enter.

6. Either enter another To-Do item or press enter again to end the list.

Using the Check List

You create a check list, using it is simple. Tapping a check box causes it to become checked. You can remove the checkmark by tapping the box again.

It's Not All Good

If you read the chapter on messaging (Chapter 3, "Messaging"), then you know that Outlook Mobile allows for the creation of to-do lists. However, One Note does not allow you to use the To-Do icon to import an Outlook To-Do list.

Controlling Indention

The desktop version of Microsoft One Note is free-form in nature, meaning you can add text, images, and other elements to any spot in the document that you like. The mobile version is not quite as accepting. You can't just tap a desired spot on the screen and then begin typing in that spot. However, that isn't to say you can't place text, images, or audio in a predetermined location.

To insert text or other items into a specific spot on the page, follow these steps:

1. Press Enter repeatedly until you reach the desired vertical location.

2. Flick the ... icon upward to reveal the submenu.

3. Use the Increase Indent and Decrease Indent options to move the cursor to the desired horizontal location.

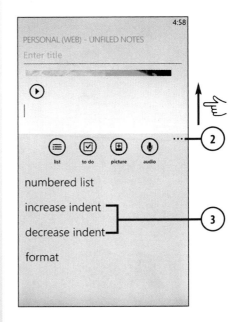

Formatting One Note Text

One Note gives you the ability to apply various visual elements to the text you type. The instructions that follow explain how to apply formatting to text that has already been typed, but you can also apply formatting to new text by picking the formatting style and then typing the text. You can format text that has already been typed by following these steps:

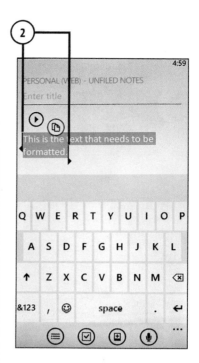

1. Double-tap a word within the block of text you want to format. This causes the word to become selected.

2. Tap and drag the arrow icons beneath the selected text to select any additional required text.

3. Flick the ... icon upward to reveal the submenu.

4. Tap Format.

Choose your desired formatting style. The available styles include

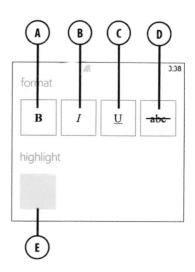

A. **Bold**

B. **Italics**

C. **Underline**

D. **Strikethrough**

E. **Highlight**

When you return to the document, tap an empty area of the screen to reveal the new formatting.

Saving a One Note Document

As you work on a One Note document, your changes are saved automatically. As such, there is no option to save your documents.

Sharing a One Note Document

You do not have the option of sharing a One Note document as you create it. If you want to share a document, follow these steps:

1. Close your document (the changes are saved automatically).

2. Open the document.

3. Tap the email icon.

4. Enter the recipient information and tap Send.

DOCUMENT REVISIONS

When you open a One Note document, the List, Picture, and Audio icons are replaced with Pin, email, and Sync icons. As such, it might at first seem that the document cannot be edited. If you want to make changes to the document, tap an empty area. The List, Picture, and Audio icons return, and you can begin revising your document.

Go Further

Excel

Although not quite as full-featured as the desktop version, the mobile version of Excel allows you to create and view spreadsheets with ease. Excel Mobile can even be used to open Excel 2010 documents, but any unsupported features that were used in the document are ignored by Excel Mobile.

Creating a New Spreadsheet

You can create a new Excel spreadsheet by following these steps:

1. Press the Start button.

2. Flick the arrow icon to access the App list.

3. Tap Office.

4. Flick the screen to access the Documents page.

5. Tap the New icon.

6. Tap Excel.

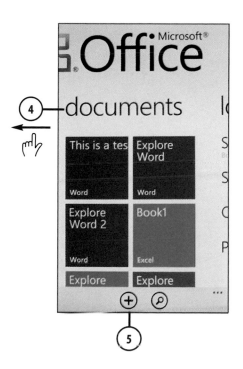

Document Templates

The procedure just outlined assumes you want to create a blank Excel spreadsheet. However, when you tap the New icon, Windows provides a number of different templates you can choose from to create preformatted spreadsheets. For example, Microsoft provides templates for tracking expenses, tracking vehicle mileage, and even a golf score card.

Adding Data to a Spreadsheet

The process of entering data into a spreadsheet is a little bit different from what you might be used to in Office 2010. In Office 2010, you can click in a cell and then type either a formula or a value. In Excel Mobile, you must tap in a cell and then tap the text field at the top of the screen before entering a value or a formula.

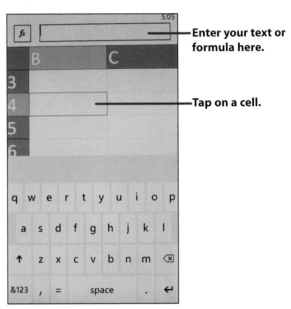

Enter your text or formula here.

Tap on a cell.

Adding a Comment to a Cell

Unlike previous versions of Excel Mobile, the Windows Phone 7 version supports the use of comments within spreadsheets. You can add a comment to a spreadsheet by following these steps:

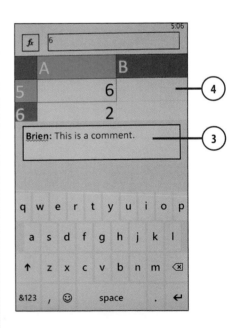

1. Tap in the cell on which you want to comment. The cell must contain text.

2. Tap on the Comment icon.

3. Enter your comment.

4. Tap on another cell to complete the process.

THE COMMENT AUTHOR

If you look at the previous figure, you notice that my name is shown before the comment. The first time you attempt to add a comment to an Office document, you are prompted to enter your name. The name you enter is displayed along with any comments that you make. If you ever want to change the name that is used, you can do so by completing these steps:

1. Press the Start button.

2. Flick the arrow icon to access the App list.

3. Scroll to the bottom of the App list and tap Settings.

4. Flick the screen to the Application Settings page.

5. Tap Office.

6. Tap User Name

7. Enter your name in the space provided.

8. Tap Done.

It's Not All Good

Adding comments and numerous other functions require you to be able to access the icon bar at the bottom of the screen. A bug in the mobile operating system causes this bar to be illusive at times. If you are tapping in cells, but the icon bar does not appear, try pressing the phone's Back button. Often times this forces the icon bar to appear.

Viewing a Comment

Even if someone added a comment to an Excel spreadsheet by using a desktop version of Excel, you can still read those comments in Excel Mobile. To do so:

1. Look for a cell with a small colored triangle in the upper right corner.

2. Tap in the cell to view the comment.

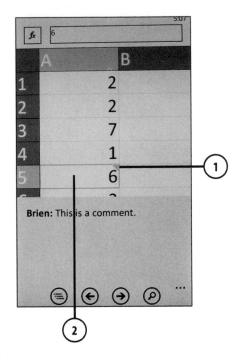

Viewing All Comments

If a spreadsheet contains multiple comments, you can view all of the comments in the entire spreadsheet by following these steps:

1. Tap in the cell containing a comment.

2. Use the Previous and Next icons to view other comments within the spreadsheet.

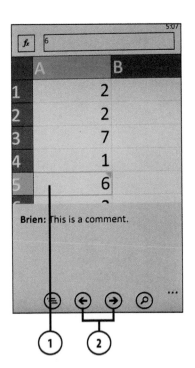

Searching a Spreadsheet

The easiest way to locate text within a large spreadsheet is to use the Search function. To do so, follow these steps:

1. Tap the Find icon.

2. Enter the text you want to search for.

3. When Excel locates a cell containing the specified text, you can use the Next icon to find additional occurrences of the text.

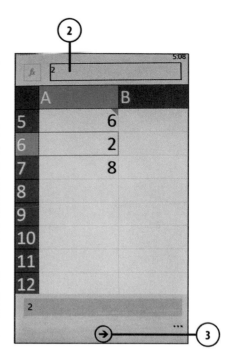

Selecting Cells

It might occasionally be necessary to select multiple cells within a spreadsheet. For example, if you want to apply formatting to a large area, it is easier to select the cells in the area that you want to format and then apply the formatting to the selected cells than to apply formatting to each cell individually. You can select multiple cells by tapping in the first cell within the range of cells you want to select and then dragging your finger until all of the desired cells have been selected.

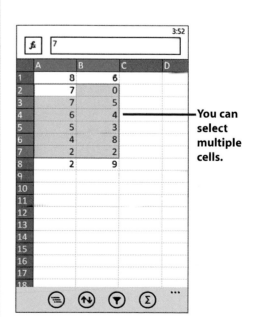

You can select multiple cells.

Go Further

SELECTED CELLS

There are a number of different actions you can perform when you select a range of cells. Any time you select a range of cells, Excel displays the Outline, Sort, Filter, and Auto Sum icons you can use to control the selected cells. However, if you flick the ... icon upward to reveal the submenu, which offers several other options.

Viewing Cell Text

Occasionally a cell might contain too much data to be able to read the cell's full contents within the confines of the current column. In these types of situations you can get Excel to show you the cell's full contents. To do so, follow these steps:

1. Tap and hold the cell you want to view.

2. Tap View Cell Text.

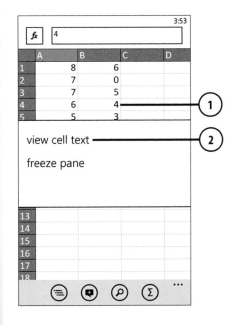

Freezing a Pane

Freezing a pane allows you to keep a range of cells on screen while you scroll the rest of the cells. For example, you might want to keep the spreadsheet's header rows on screen while you view data further down the spreadsheet. You can freeze a portion of the spreadsheet by following these steps:

1. Tap and hold a cell in the row that you want to freeze.

2. Tap Freeze Pane.

Frozen Cells

You will notice in the figure that a blue line indicates the cells that are frozen. When you decide to unfreeze the cells, you can do so by tapping and holding a cell above the blue line and tapping the Unfreeze Pane option.

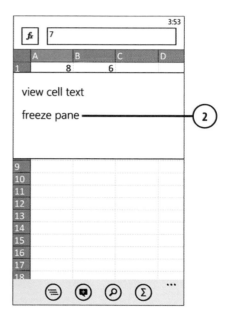

Applying Formatting Options

Excel Mobile allows you to apply a number of different text effects to cells within your spreadsheet. To modify the text style, follow these steps:

1. Select the cells to which you wish to apply a text effect.

2. Flick the ... icon upward to reveal the submenu.

3. Tap Format Cell.

4. Tap the formatting option that you wish to apply. The available formatting options include

   A. Bold

   B. Italics

   C. Underline

   D. Date

   E. Currency

   F. Percentage

   G. Font Color

   H. Fill Color

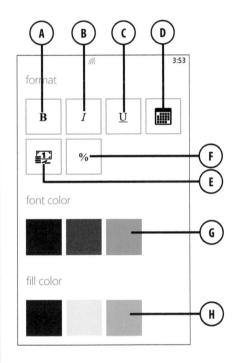

Sorting a Column

Excel Mobile makes it easy to sort a column of data either alphabetically or numerically. To sort a column, follow these steps:

1. Tap the header for the column that you wish to sort. This causes the entire column to be selected.

2. Tap the Sort icon.

3. Verify that the Sort By field lists the appropriate column.

4. Tap the Sort Order field and choose either the Ascending or Descending option.

5. Tap the More Options button.

6. Tap the Exclude Header Row check box if necessary.

7. Tap Done to complete the sort.

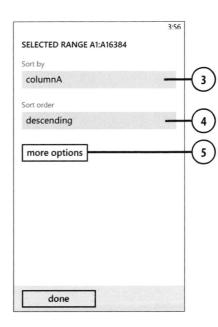

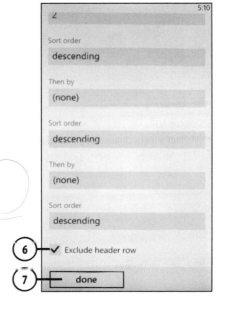

Multilevel Sorting

Just as you can sort a single column of data, Excel Mobile also gives you the ability to sort multiple columns. You can perform a multilevel sort by following these steps:

1. Select the columns that you want to include in the sort.

2. Tap the Sort icon.

3. Verify that the Sort By field lists the appropriate column.

4. Tap the Sort Order field and choose either the Ascending or the Descending option.

5. Tap the More Options button.

6. Tap the Then By field.

7. Choose your secondary sort option.

8. Tap the Sort Order field.

9. Choose whether you want to perform the secondary sort in ascending or descending order.

10. Tap the check box if you want to exclude the header row from the sort.

11. Tap Done.

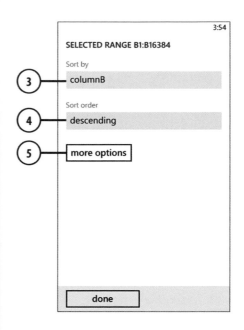

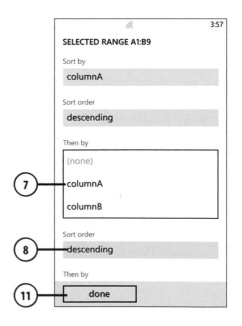

Filtering Cell Contents

Excel Mobile contains a powerful filtering mechanism that you can use
to hide all of the spreadsheet data
except for the specific data that you
are interested in. You can filter
spreadsheet data by completing
these steps:

1. Tap on a cell on the top row of
   the spreadsheet.

2. Tap the Filter icon.

3. Tap the icon in the top cell of the
   column that you want to filter.

4. Tap the desired filter option. All
   data will be hidden except for the
   filter you have selected.

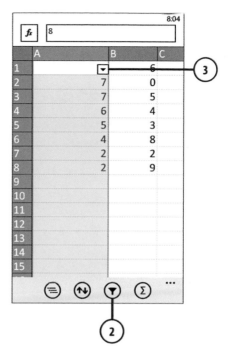

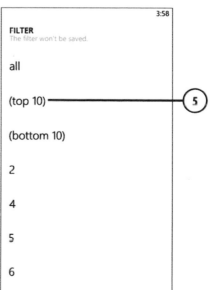

Undo and Redo

Any time you are working on a spreadsheet on a mobile device touch screen, it is easy to make a mistake. Thankfully, Excel Mobile contains an Undo and a Redo function. You can access Undo and Redo by flicking the ... icon upward to reveal the submenu. Keep in mind that Undo and Redo might be grayed out if your last action wasn't something that can be undone (such as applying a filter).

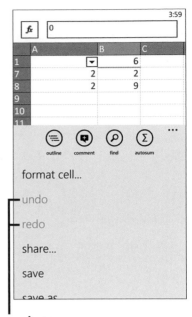

You can undo or redo various operations.

Charting

In spite of its simple interface, Excel Mobile allows you to add charts to a spreadsheet. To do so, follow these steps:

1. Select a range of cells containing the data that you want to chart.

2. Flick the ... icon upward to reveal the submenu.

3. Tap Insert Chart.

4. Tap the type of chart that you want to insert.

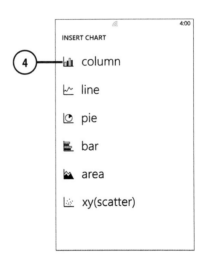

Accessing Charts and Sheets

In Microsoft Excel 2010, a single workbook can contain multiple sheets, which are accessible through tabs at the bottom of the screen. Excel Mobile also supports the use of multiple sheets, but the tabs do not exist. Instead, tap the Outline icon. When you do, Excel displays a list of all of the sheets and charts that make up the current workbook. You can access a sheet or chart simply by tapping it.

You can view the various sheets and charts that make up the spreadsheet.

Saving a Spreadsheet

You can save your spreadsheet at any time by completing these steps:

1. Tap in an empty cell within the spreadsheet.

2. Flick the … icon upward to reveal the submenu.

3. Flick the submenu upward to reveal the lower portion.

4. Tap either Save or Save As.

5. If prompted, enter a file name.

6. Tap the Save To field.

7. Choose the destination to which you want to save the file.

8. Tap Save.

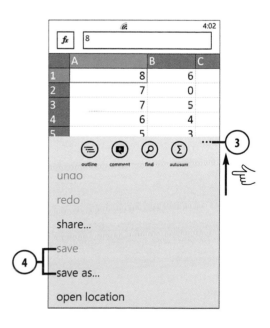

Sharing a Spreadsheet

You can send a spreadsheet by email by completing these steps:

1. Tap in a cell.

2. Flick the … icon upward to reveal the submenu.

3. Tap Share.

4. If prompted, choose the mailbox you want to use to send the spreadsheet.

5. Enter the recipient information for the email message.

6. Tap Send.

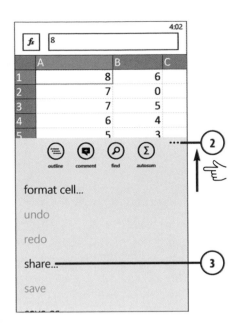

Fitting Text

Sometimes you might find that a cell is not wide enough to display all of the text within it. When this happens there are two things you can do to make the text visible. One option is to perform an auto fit. An auto fit expands the width of the column to accommodate the text.

The other option is to wrap the text so that it fits within the current column width.

You can access both of these options by tapping and holding the cell at the top of the column you want to adjust. The full column is selected, and a menu provides the options to auto fit or to wrap the text within the selected column.

The Autofit and Wrap Text options help data to better fit within the spreadsheet's cells.

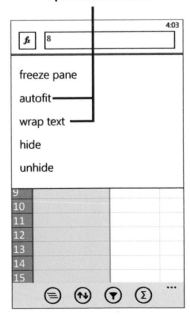

Hiding Columns

There is a limited amount of space on the Windows Phone screen, and sometimes it might be easier to work with a spreadsheet if you can hide columns that you don't need at the moment. To do so, follow these steps:

1. Tap and hold the column you want to hide.

2. Choose the Hide option from the menu when it appears.

Revealing Hidden Columns

You can reveal a hidden column at any time by tapping and holding the top row of the spreadsheet and then choosing the Unhide option from the resulting menu.

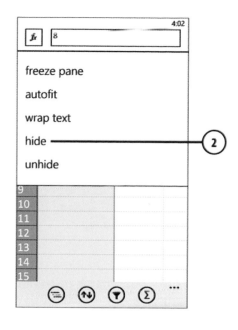

Auto Sum

Even though Excel Mobile supports the same formulas as Excel 2010, you might occasionally want to perform a quick calculation without having to write a formula. This is where the Auto Sum icon comes into play. If you select a range of cells and then tap the Auto Sum icon, Excel shows you the sum of the values within the selected cells as well as a few other stats such as the minimum, maximum, and average values.

Autosum automatically performs a number of calculations on the selected cells.

Word

Of all the apps included with Windows Phone, perhaps none is more useful than Microsoft Word Mobile. This app allows you to create, view, and edit Microsoft Word documents while you are on the go.

Creating a New Word Document

The technique for creating a new Word document is very similar to that of creating an Excel document. To create a Word document, follow these steps:

1. Press the Start button.

2. Flick the arrow icon to access the App list screen.

3. Tap Office.

4. Flick the screen to access the Documents page.

5. Tap the New icon.

6. Tap Word

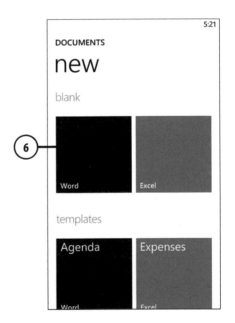

The Microsoft Word Interface

As you can see in the figure, Word Mobile resembles a watered down version of Notepad. It consists of a blank screen, a keyboard, and a few icons. Fortunately, all is not what it seems. There is much more to Word Mobile than meets the eye. This chapter explains in detail which features are available through Word Mobile. For right now, though, following are the elements present on the screen when you create a new document:

A. **Current time**

B. **Document body**

C. **On screen keyboard**

D. **Outline icon**

E. **Comment icon**

F. **Find icon**

G. **Format icon**

H. **Submenu icon**

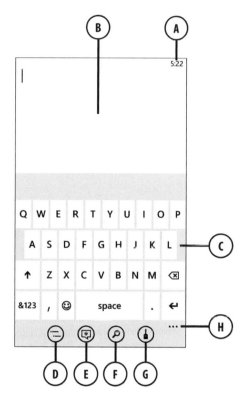

Copy and Paste

Windows Phone devices fully support the use of Copy and Paste within Microsoft Word and other apps. To use Copy and Paste within a Word document, follow these steps.

1. Tap on a word that is to be included within the text you want to copy.

2. When the word is selected, drag the arrows beneath the word to select any additional words you want to include.

3. Tap the Copy icon.

4. Tap the Edit icon.

5. Tap the location within the document where you want to paste the newly copied contents.

6. Tap the Paste icon.

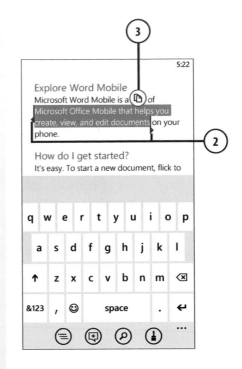

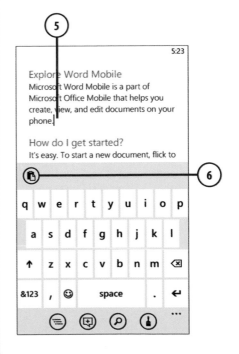

Applying Text Effects

As you enter text into a Word document, you have the option of formatting that text using various styles. For instance, you can make text bold face, or you can highlight it. To do so, follow these steps:

1. Move the cursor to the appropriate location within the document or select the text to which you want to apply the effect.

2. Tap the Format icon.

3. Tap the effect you want to apply, choosing from

   A. Bold

   B. Italics

   C. Underline

   D. Strikethrough

   E. Superscript

   F. Subscript

   G. Highlight

   H. Font Color

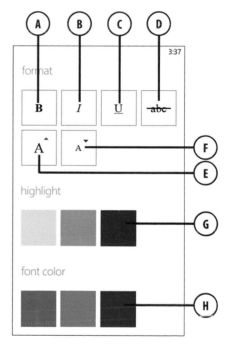

Locating Text Within a Document

When viewing or editing longer word documents it can sometimes be helpful to be able to search for key words or phrases within the document. If you need to locate specific words or phrases, follow these steps:

1. Tap the Find icon.

2. Enter your search text.

3. Word marks the first occurrence of the search text.

4. You can find additional occurrences by clicking the Next icon.

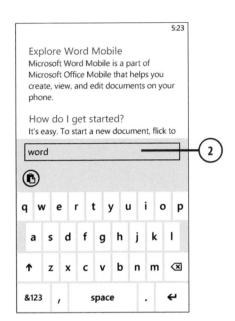

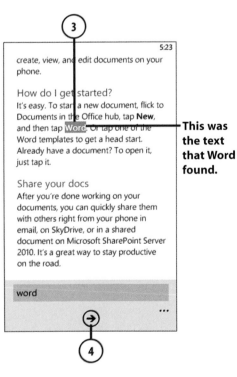

This was the text that Word found.

Adding a Comment

For many years the desktop version of Microsoft Word has allowed comments to be entered into a document. However, this feature has never existed in Word Mobile until now. If you want to add a comment to a document, you can do so by following these steps:

1. Select the location for the comment within the document.

2. Tap the Comment icon.

3. Type your comment.

4. Tap the selected text to complete the process.

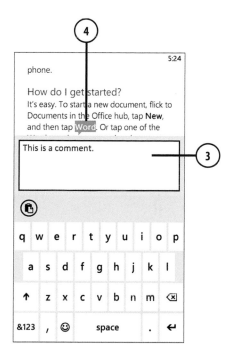

Viewing a Comment

If you receive a Word document that contains comments, you can view those comments by following these steps:

1. Locate the text for which a comment has been made. The commented text is flagged with a comment icon.

2. Double-tap on the commented text.

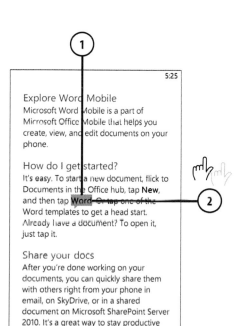

3. The comment is displayed at the bottom of the screen.

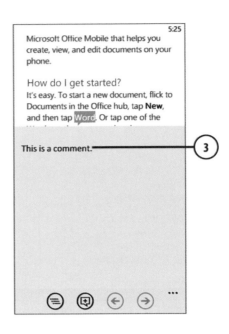

Documents with Multiple Comments

Often, documents contain multiple comments. You can move from one comment to the next without having to locate each individual comment within the document. To do so, follow these steps:

1. Locate the first comment within the document.

2. Double-tap the commented text to view the comment.

3. Tap the Next icon to view the next comment.

4. If necessary, tap the Previous icon to view the previous comment.

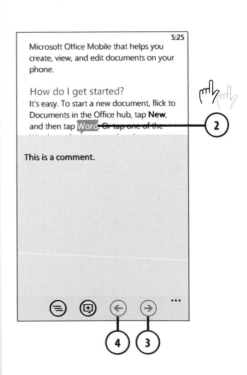

Sending the Document

After you create or edit a document, you might want to email it to yourself or to others. To do so, follow these steps:

1. Swipe the ... icon upward to reveal the submenu.

2. Tap Share.

3. If your document needs to be saved, you are prompted to do so now.

4. You might be prompted to select the email account you want to use.

5. When Outlook opens, specify who the document should be sent to.

6. Enter a subject line for the message.

7. Add any necessary body text.

8. Tap the Send icon.

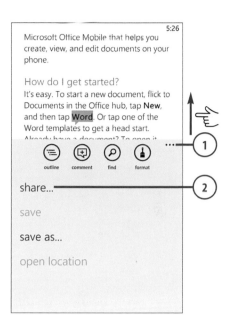

Saving the Document

You can save a Word document at any time by following these steps:

1. Swipe the … icon upward to reveal the submenu.

2. Tap Save or Save As.

3. If the document has not been previously saved (or if you chose the Save As option), you are prompted to enter a filename and a destination.

4. Tap Save.

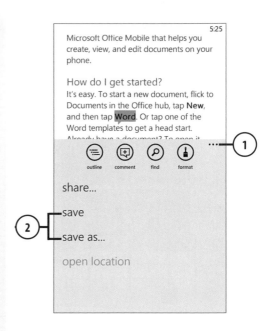

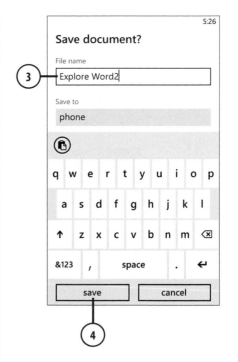

5. The next time you access the Office hub, the document appears within the Documents list.

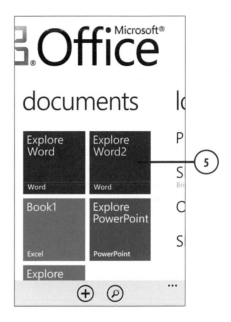

It's Not All Good

Although Word Mobile is suitable for light editing, it is missing a couple of crucial features that would be required for composing any document of significant length. For starters, Word is missing the Undo/Redo option. These options existed in the original Windows Phone 7 release, but for some reason Microsoft chose to remove them from Windows Phone 7.5. The Undo/Redo feature has been removed from One Note as well.

The other crucial feature missing from Word Mobile is a spell check. Word does, however, take some steps to prevent misspellings within your documents. An Auto Correct feature automatically corrects suspected typos, and like Office 2010, Word Mobile underlines misspelled words in red. However, the Auto Correct feature has a bad habit of correcting things that aren't actually wrong (in essence introducing mistakes into your document), and there is no option to spell check the entire document.

PowerPoint

Windows Phone lets you watch PowerPoint presentations right on your phone. You even have the ability to open PowerPoint documents, make any necessary changes, and send the presentation to others. You can send a PowerPoint presentation through email, or you can upload it to a SharePoint workspace.

Its Not All Good

For some reason, Windows Phone 7 lacks the ability to create new PowerPoint presentations. The phone has no trouble creating new Word, Excel, and OneNote documents, but for some reason this essential feature was omitted from PowerPoint.

Opening a PowerPoint Document

Although PowerPoint Mobile does not allow you to create new documents, you can open existing presentations and edit them. To open a PowerPoint document, follow these steps:

1. Tap the Start button.

2. Flick the Arrow icon to access the App list.

3. Tap Office.

4. Flick the screen to access the Documents page.

5. Tap the PowerPoint document you want to open.

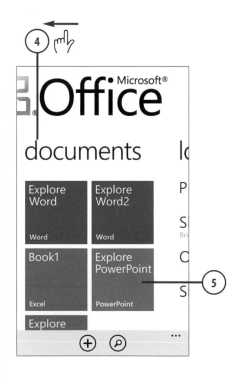

Emailed Documents

Although the preceding example dealt with opening a document that is already on your phone, you can also open PowerPoint documents as email attachments.

Viewing PowerPoint Slides

Windows Phone always displays PowerPoint slides in landscape format regardless of the phone's orientation. You can view the previous or next slide simply by flicking the display left or right (with the top of the slide facing up).

When you open a PowerPoint document, the following items are displayed on the screen:

A. Current slide

B. Edit icon

C. Notes icon

D. Outline icon

E. Submenu icon

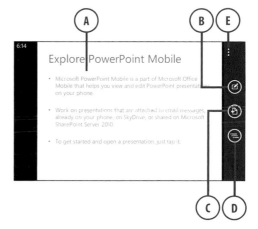

THE HIDDEN ICON BAR

To save space on the device's screen, PowerPoint has a tendency to hide the icon bar. If this happens, you can reveal the icon bar by orienting the phone so that the top of the slide is facing up and then tapping the empty margin to the right of the slide.

Go Further

Viewing a Specific Slide

If you want to view or edit a specific slide, you don't have to go through every slide in the presentation to access it. You can go to the desired slide directly. To do so, follow these steps:

1. Tap the Outline icon.

2. Tap the listing for the slide you want to view.

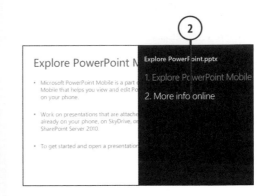

Adding Notes to a Slide

PowerPoint Mobile supports adding speaker notes to your slides. To add a note to a slide, follow these steps:

1. Go to the slide you want to add the note to.

2. Tap the Notes icon.

3. Compose your notes.

4. Tap the Done icon.

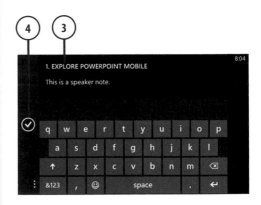

Viewing Slide Notes

You can view or edit the speaker notes that go with a slide by following these steps:

1. Tap the Outline icon to reveal the list of slides. Slides containing notes include a Notes icon.

2. Tap the Notes icon for the slide you are interested in.

3. When you are done reading or editing the notes, tap a blank area of the screen and then tap the Done icon.

Editing a Slide

PowerPoint Mobile offers limited options for editing slides. Before you can begin the editing process, you must put PowerPoint Mobile into Edit mode. To do so, follow these steps:

1. Navigate to the slide that you want to edit.

2. Tap the Edit icon.

Selecting a Text Box

When PowerPoint is in Edit Mode, the top text box is selected by default. You can choose another text box by tapping the Next icon.

The top text box is selected by default.

Tap the Next icon to select a different text box.

Editing Slide Text

When a text box has been selected, you can edit it by tapping in the text box. The text from the text box is displayed within an editor you can use to make any changes. When you finish, tap the Done icon.

The text box editor is very bare bones.

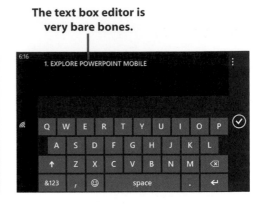

It's Not All Good

PowerPoint Mobile has no capacity for editing text styles or for adding other visual elements (such as images) to a document. When you edit a text box, your edits are done on a plain black and white screen in plain text. However, any changes that you make will adopt the style of the selected text box.

Moving a Slide

PowerPoint Mobile allows you to move a slide to another location within the document. To do so, complete these steps.

1. While in Edit Mode, flick the ... icon to the left to reveal the submenu.

2. Tap Move Slide.

3. Choose the location within the document where you want the slide moved.

4. Tap Done.

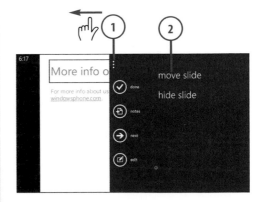

Hiding a Slide

PowerPoint Mobile also gives you
the option of hiding a slide. To do so,
follow these steps:

1. While in Edit mode, flick the …
   icon to the left to reveal the submenu.

2. Tap Hide Slide.

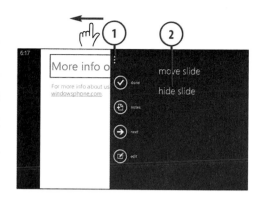

Unhiding a Slide

You can unhide a hidden slide at
any time by accessing the slide in
Edit mode, flicking the … icon to
the left to reveal the submenu,
and choosing the Unhide Slide
option.

Leaving Edit Mode

When you are done editing a slide,
you can exit Edit mode by tapping
the Done icon.

Saving the Document

To save your PowerPoint presentation, complete the following steps:

1. Make sure that PowerPoint is not
   in Edit mode.

2. Flick the … icon to the left to
   reveal the submenu.

3. Tap either Save or Save As.

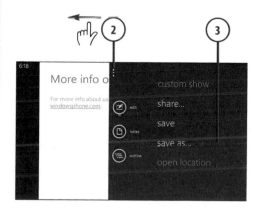

4. If you choose the Save As option, you are prompted to provide a file name and a destination.

5. Tap Save.

6. The next time you access the Office Hub, your PowerPoint presentation will be available from the Documents list.

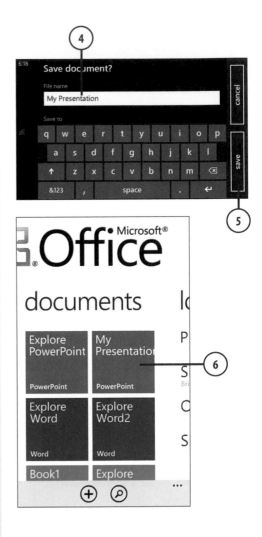

Sending the Document

PowerPoint Mobile gives you the option of emailing your presentation without leaving PowerPoint. To do so, follow these steps:

1. Make sure that PowerPoint is not in Edit mode.

2. Flick the … icon to the left to access the submenu.

3. Tap Share.

4. If the PowerPoint presentation has not yet been saved, you are prompted to save your changes.

5. If prompted, select the email account you want to use to send the document.

6. When prompted, enter the recipient's email address.

7. Add a subject line and any necessary text.

8. Tap Send.

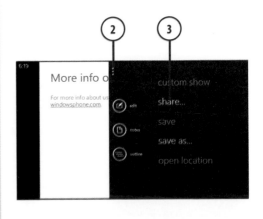

Locations

Windows Phone 7.5 devices allow Office documents to be saved in a variety of locations. In fact, the Office hub contains a Locations page you can use to access documents that are stored in various locations. The locations available to you include

• Phone

• Office 365

• SharePoint

• SkyDrive

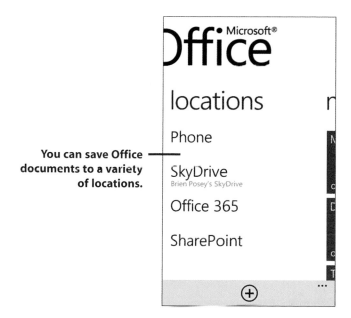

You can save Office documents to a variety of locations.

Phone

Another option on the Locations screen is Phone. If you tap the Phone option, Windows takes you to the Documents page, which shows a list of the documents that are stored on your phone.

Office documents can be saved directly to the phone.

Office 365

Windows Phone is also designed to be able to access documents that are stored within Office 365 (a Microsoft cloud service). If you tap the Office 365 option, you should be taken directly to the SharePoint document library for your Office 365 subscription.

One thing to keep in mind is that Office 365 must be set up before it will be accessible from your phone. The way Windows Phone 7.5 devices connect to Office 365 is through Outlook. The Email+Accounts setting (which was covered in Chapter 3) contains an option to link Outlook to an Office 365 Server.

If you have not previously connected your Windows Phone to an Office 365 server, then tapping the Office 365 option causes a screen to be displayed telling you that your phone must be set up to connect to Office 365. Tapping the corresponding Set Up button takes you to the Email+Accounts screen.

Windows Phone 7 supports Office 365, but it must be set up before you can use it.

SharePoint

Windows Phone is designed to provide access to SharePoint sites directly through the Office hub. By doing so, it is possible to access Office documents that are stored in SharePoint document libraries.

It's Not All Good

Unfortunately, SharePoint support through the Office hub is one feature that is definitely not ready for prime time. To connect the Office hub to a SharePoint site, there are several conditions that must be met. Otherwise when you try to connect to the SharePoint server, you receive an authentication error.

If you navigate to the Office hub's Locations page and tap SharePoint, you are prompted to enter the URL for your SharePoint Server. However, connectivity is only possible if the SharePoint server meets a number of criteria including

- The SharePoint site must be running SharePoint 2010.

- SharePoint must be externally accessible via Fully Qualified Domain Name.

- The SharePoint site must be configured to support SSL encryption.

- The certificate that is used to facilitate SSL encryption must be added to the Windows Phone device. The device lacks a certificate manager, but it is possible to email yourself the certificate and then install the certificate by opening the message's attachment.

- SharePoint must be configured to use Forms Based Authentication.

So what's the problem? Well, configuring a SharePoint 2010 server to meet these conditions is a tall order. SharePoint 2010 was designed to use NTLM authentication, which is not supported by Windows Phone. You can enable Forms Based Authentication for SharePoint 2010, but doing so is not a simple matter, and it violates Microsoft's stated best practices for SharePoint.

If you (or the network administrator at your company) want to try to configure SharePoint so that users can link to it from the Office hub, Microsoft provides some important technical details in a series of posts at: http://social.technet.microsoft.com/Forums/en-US/sharepoint2010setup/thread/f95c7008-ed48-4a22-b3f4-a6beac664860/

A SharePoint Workaround

If you can't access SharePoint document libraries directly through the Office hub, there is a workaround. In the screen shot shown next, you will notice that just beneath the URL field there is a message saying to Tap Here to Import SharePoint Links Instead. Tapping this link takes you to another screen that asks for your SharePoint server's URL. This time however, when you enter the URL, your SharePoint site is open in Internet Explorer. Because some SharePoint sites can be a bit cluttered, Windows Phone is designed to open the mobile version of a SharePoint site.

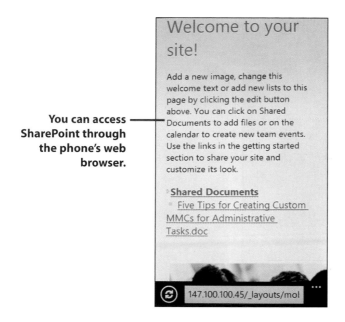

You can access SharePoint through the phone's web browser.

Although accessing SharePoint through a browser might not be as conven-ient as going through the Office hub, it is possible to add a SharePoint URL to your favorites list or even to pin the site to your Start screen for easy access. To do so, open the site in Internet Explorer and then tap the Add icon to add the site to your favorites list. If you want to pin the site to your Start screen then flick the ... icon upward to reveal Internet Explorer's submenu and then tap Pin to Start.

SkyDrive

The preferred location for storing Office documents is Microsoft's SkyDrive. If you tap the SkyDrive option on the Locations page, Windows displays the contents of your SkyDrive. You can flick between pages containing your documents and shared documents.

You can access documents while on the go by storing them in your Sky Drive.

Changing Office Mobile Settings

There are a few different configuration options that you can set for Office Mobile. You can access these configuration settings by following these steps:

1. Press the Start button.

2. Flick the screen to access the App list.

3. Tap Settings.

4. Flick the screen to the Applications page.

5. Tap Office.

The settings screen for Office contains several different settings including

A. **User Name**—This is the name that appears next to any comments that you make within an Office document. If you create a new Office document from your phone, the User Name is used as the document author.

B. **Open SharePoint Links in the Office Hub**—Controls whether or not SharePoint links are accessible through the Office hub.

C. **UAG Server**—The UAG Server option is used to provide a path and credentials for accessing a SharePoint Server through a ForeFront Unified Access Gateway.

D. **Reset Office**—The Reset Office button deletes all of your Office documents and resets Office to its default settings.

Access Xbox Live, right from your phone!

Those who are into XBOX gaming are sure to love the phone's XBOX Live hub. In this chapter, you will learn how to use it to interact with your XBOX Live account in much the same way that you do from your gaming console.

XBOX Gaming

One of the things that makes Windows Phone really stand out from competing devices such as the iPhone is that Windows Phone has XBOX Live built into the phone. You won't be able to use your phone to play XBOX 360 games, but you can access your XBOX Live profile through the phone and can download a wide variety of games from the marketplace.

Accessing the XBOX Live Hub

You can access the XBOX Live Hub directly through the Start screen by tapping the XBOX Live icon.

The Start screen
provides direct
access to XBOX Live.

In the event that the XBOX Live icon gets removed from the Start menu, you can access the XBOX Live hub by flicking the arrow icon to access the App List and tapping the Games icon.

You can launch Xbox
Live from the App
list.

Connecting an XBOX Live Account

The first thing you should do when you go into the XBOX Live hub for the first time is to connect your XBOX Live Account. If you have an XBOX 360 gaming console, you can connect your phone to your existing XBOX Live account. Otherwise, you can create a brand new account directly through the phone.

Joining XBOX Live

You have several different options for joining XBOX Live. You can create an XBOX Live account directly through your phone, or you can do it from your XBOX 360 console or from an Internet enabled PC. You can set up an XBOX Live account from your phone by following these steps:

1. Press the Start button.

2. Tap the XBOX Live Button.

3. Flick the screen to reach the XBOX Live page.

4. Tap the Join XBOX Live to Play with Friends or Sign In.

Xbox Live Accounts

The phone must be connected to a Windows Live account before you can join XBOX Live.

5. When prompted, specify your country or region and your date of birth.

6. Tap Accept.

7. After your Windows Live account is created, make note of your Gamertag. Your friends will need your gamertag to find you online on XBOX Live.

8. Tap Done, and you are returned to XBOX Live. You are automatically signed in using your new XBOX Live account.

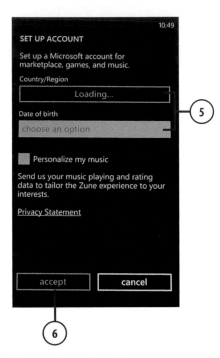

Be sure to make note of your gamer tag.

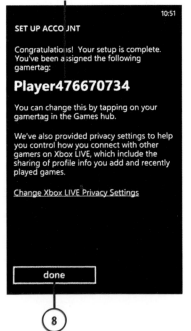

Windows Live

XBOX Live accounts are linked to Windows Live Accounts. You should have already set up a Windows Live account when you initially configured the phone, and the instructions in this section assume you are already signed into Windows Live.

You are automatically signed in with your new gamer tag.

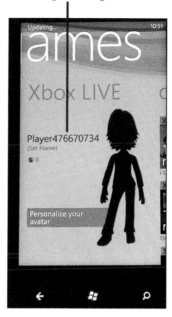

Using an Existing XBOX Live Account

XBOX Live accounts are linked to Windows Live accounts. Therefore, if you provided Windows Phone with your Windows Live ID during the initial setup process, you won't have to do anything to get the phone to recognize your XBOX Live account. The phone uses it automatically.

If you haven't yet made the phone aware of your Windows Live ID, you can do so while setting up your XBOX Live account. To link your XBOX Live account to your phone, follow these steps:

1. Press the Start button.

2. Tap the XBOX Live icon.

3. On the XBOX Live screen, tap I Already Have an XBOX Live Account.

4. You see a message telling you that a Windows Live ID is required. Tap Sign In.

5. Windows displays a warning message telling you that the Windows Live ID that you provide must be the one you will use with XBOX and Zune. Tap Next to clear this warning.

Windows Live ID required

To use this feature, you'll need to sign in with a Windows Live ID. If you don't have one, we'll help you create one. It should only take a moment.

sign in   cancel

Player

⊙ 0

Join Xbox LIVE to play with friends

I already have an Xbox LIVE account

④

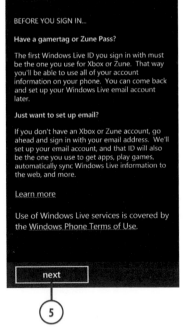

BEFORE YOU SIGN IN...

Have a gamertag or Zune Pass?

The first Windows Live ID you sign in with must be the one you use for Xbox or Zune. That way you'll be able to use all of your account information on your phone. You can come back and set up your Windows Live email account later.

Just want to set up email?

If you don't have an Xbox or Zune account, go ahead and sign in with your email address. We'll set up your email account, and that ID will also be the one you use to get apps, play games, automatically sync Windows Live information to the web, and more.

Learn more

Use of Windows Live services is covered by the Windows Phone Terms of Use.

next

⑤

6. Enter your Windows Live ID and password and tap Sign In.

Your XBOX Live Account
Step 3 in the instructions just delineated is to tap the I Already Have an XBOX Live Account option. However, this option only exists if the phone has not automatically detected your account. Otherwise, your Gamertag is displayed along with your avatar.

The XBOX Live Hub

The XBOX Live hub consists of four screens. You can access the various screens by flicking the screen to the left or to the right. Here is a summary of the screens and their functions:

- **XBOX Live**—This screen displays your avatar and your Windows Live ID.

- **Requests**—The Requests screen shows you any existing game invites or turn notifications.

- **Collection**—The Collection screen provides access to your game collection.

- **Spotlight**—The Spotlight screen shows games that are currently being promoted.

XBOX LIVE ACCOUNTS

Microsoft offers three different types of XBOX Live accounts. A basic XBOX Live account is free and allows you to preview games through free demos and to download new games or game add-ons. Like all XBOX Live accounts, a free account allows you to create and customize an avatar and access Zune movies. Additionally, you can use the free account to chat with friends.

If you want more than just the basics, you can upgrade to the XBOX Live Gold package for $9.99 per month or $59.99 per year. The gold package offers all of the same functionality as the free account but also offers movies from Netflix, sports from ESPN, and music from Zune. You can also use the Gold plan to access Video Kinect and Facebook on your TV through an XBOX 360 console. Of course the primary benefit to an XBOX Live Gold subscription is online gaming with your friends.

Microsoft also offers a family plan for $99.99 per year, which includes four separate XBOX Live Gold accounts and a reporting function that can be used to monitor how each of the included XBOX Live accounts is being used.

Creating or Editing Your XBOX Live Profile

The XBOX Live Extras give you the full ability to edit your XBOX Live profile directly from your phone. To edit (or create) your profile, follow these steps:

1. Press the Start button.

2. Tap the XBOX Live button.

3. Flick the screen to access the XBOX Live page.

4. Tap the Profile icon.

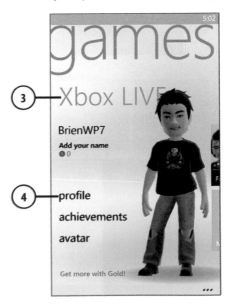

5. Tap the Edit icon.

6. Tap in and the populate each of the various profile fields.

7. Tap Save.

Changing Your Gamer Tag

The Profile screen contains a series of links related to modifying your XBOX Live gamertag. However, these links merely take you to a website with instructions for gamer tag modification. There is no functionality built into the phone for changing a gamertag.

Profile Privacy

By default nobody is able to view your profile information. The next section deals with modifying your privacy settings so that you can control who sees your profile information.

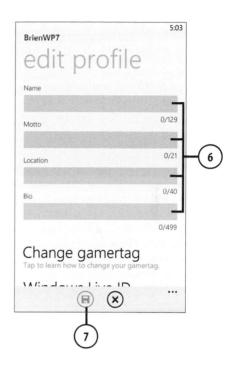

BrienWP7   5:03

edit profile

Name

                                              0/129
Motto

                                              0/21
Location

                                              0/40
Bio

                                              0/499

Change gamertag
Tap to learn how to change your gamertag.

6

7

PROFILE FIELDS

There are several different pieces of information you can include in your profile:

- **Name**—Your name or handle

- **Motto**—An optional catch phrase to be displayed with your name

- **Location**—Your geographical location

- **Bio**—A little bit about you

It's Not All Good

There is an option at the bottom of the Edit Profile screen you can use to change the Windows Live ID that is associated with your gamertag. This is not an option to be used lightly. Associating a Windows Live ID with your phone is a semi-permanent operation. If you associate your gamertag with a different Windows Live ID, you will have to reset the phone to its factory defaults so that you can begin using the alternate Windows Live ID (and your gamertag). This means erasing all of the configuration settings and data (music, videos, pictures, games, and so on) that is stored in your phone.

Adjust Your Privacy Settings

When you initially create your XBOX Live profile, various privacy settings keep it from being displayed to anyone. You can adjust the privacy settings for your profile by completing these steps:

1. Press the Start button.

2. Tap the XBOX Live button.

3. Flick the screen to access the XBOX Live page.

4. Flick the ... icon upward to access the submenu.

5. Tap Settings.

6. Use the Settings screen to enable or disable the phone's ability to connect to XBOX Live, sync game requests, and show game alerts.

7. Tap the XBOX Live Privacy Settings link.

8. Configure the desired privacy settings.

9. Tap the Save icon.

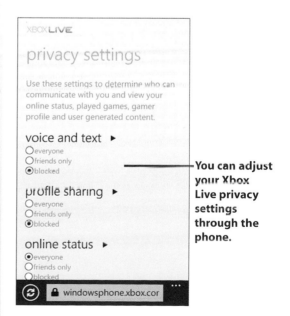

You can adjust your Xbox Live privacy settings through the phone.

PRIVACY SETTINGS

For each of the available privacy settings, there are three different options, which are Everyone, Friends Only, or Blocked.

The individual settings you can control include

Voice and Text—The Voice and Text setting controls who can communicate with you using voice or text on XBOX Live. This setting applies to voice and text chat as well as messaging and game invites. It is worth noting that this setting is blocked by default, which could prevent you from receiving messages and game invites.

Profile Sharing—The profile sharing option controls who can see your profile. A profile contains more than just your name, motto, location, and bio. It also includes your gaming history, achievements, and in some cases even a picture.

Online Status—The Online Status setting controls who can see your online status, which reflects the last time that you were online, your current or previous online activity, what you are playing right now, and your availability to play with others.

Member Content—This setting controls whether or not you will see member created content within games. Member content includes images, text, and custom game content. The setting does not impact your ability to download indie games.

Game History—The game history setting controls who is allowed to see your gaming history and your achievements.

Friends List—The Friends list setting controls who can see your friends list. Remember that granting access to your friends list grants access to your friend's profiles.

The privacy settings are configured through a web interface rather than through a native Windows Phone 7.5 feature. As such, it can take up to four hours for changes to your privacy settings to take effect.

Customizing Your Avatar

If you have ever used an XBOX 360 gaming console, you know that when you create your initial profile, you set up an avatar to go along with it. Your avatar is a cartoon character that represents you online. The XBOX 360 has numerous options for creating and customizing an avatar and most—if not all—of these options are also available on Windows Phone 7.5. To customize your avatar, follow these steps:

1. Press the Start button.

2. Tap the XBOX Live button.

3. Flick the screen to access the XBOX Live page.

4. Tap the Avatar link.

5. If you have never customized your avatar through your phone before, you might see a message telling you that you must install a free app called XBOX Live Extras. If you see this message, tap the Install button to install the necessary components.

6. The avatar customization screen is similar to what is available on the XBOX 360 console. There is a Change My Style option and a Change My Features option, as well as a link to the Marketplace.

7. Tap Change My Style.

8. Tap the icon corresponding to the clothing or accessories you want to customize.

9. Make your customizations and then tap the Back button.

10. Tap Change My Features.

The Avatar screen is very similar to what you see on the Xbox 360 gaming console.

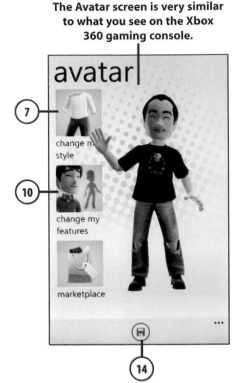

style

11. Choose the body feature you want to customize.

12. Each feature provides you with many different options to choose from.

13. When you are done, tap the Back button to return to the main Avatar screen.

14. Tap Save.

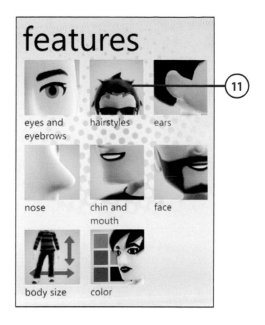

Individual features are highly customizable.

Achievements

The XBOX Live Extras software can display your gaming achievements in a manner similar to the way that your achievements are displayed on an XBOX 360 gaming console. You can view your achievements by following these steps:

1. Press the Start button.

2. Tap the XBOX Live button.

3. Flick the screen to access the XBOX Live page.

4. Tap Achievements.

The Achievements screen lists your Xbox gaming achievements.

You can access more detailed information about an individual game by tapping it. Doing so provides a detailed list of achievements. In some cases this screen also tells you what you need to do in order to accomplish certain achievements.

Tapping on an individual game provides additional detail about your progress in that game.

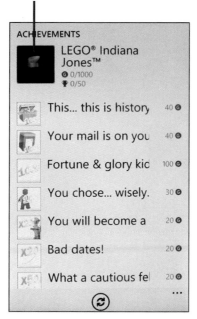

Friends

XBOX LIve is designed to be a social gaming environment in which you can compete against your friends. As such, the XBOX 360 gaming console allows you to compile a list of your friends. By doing so, you are able to easily connect with them simply by picking a name from your friends list.

Accessing Your Friends List

Your friends list is also accessible from Windows Phone by using the Windows Live Extras software. To access your Friends list, follow these steps:

1. Press the Start button.

2. Tap the XBOX Live button.

3. Flick the screen to access the XBOX Live page.

4. Tap the Achievements link.

5. When the Achievements page loads, flick the screen to access the Friends page.

The Friends screen organizes your list of friends based on who is currently online. Friends who are not online at the moment are listed in the Offline section, along with the date when they were most recently online.

Seeing Friends' Profiles

The XBOX Live Essentials software lets you access your friends' XBOX Live profiles directly through your phone. To do so, follow these steps:

1. Press the Start button.

2. Tap the XBOX Live button.

3. Flick the screen to access the XBOX Live page.

4. Tap the Achievements link.

5. When the Achievements page loads, flick the screen to access the Friends page.

6. Tap on the friend whose profile you want to view.

Friend's Profiles

When you tap a friend to view their profile, the profile is spread across several pages you can flick between. The profile pages include

Profile—Displays your friend's avatar and includes an option for sending a message to your friend.

Recent Games—Displays all of the games that your friend has played recently.

Compare—A comparison between the games your friend has played and the games you have played.

Bio—Your friend's bio.

Comparing Achievements

Just as the XBOX Live Essentials software allows you to view your own gaming accomplishments, you can also compare your accomplishments against a friend's. To compare gaming accomplishments, follow these steps:

1. Press the Start button.

2. Tap the XBOX Live button.

3. Flick the screen to access the XBOX Live page.

4. Tap the Achievements link.

5. When the Achievements page loads, flick the screen to access the Friends page.

6. Tap on the friend whose achievements you want to view.

7. When your friend's profile is displayed, flick the screen to access the Compare screen.

You can view your friend's XBOX Live profiles directly through your phone.

The Compare screen provides a summary of the achievements for your entire game collection. For detailed achievement information about a specific game, tap the game.

Missing Achievements

The XBOX Live privacy settings have a big impact on what achievements are actually displayed. If you are having difficulty getting the achievements comparison to work correctly, be sure to read the section on privacy settings later in this chapter.

You can compare level by level achievements for a single game.

Adding a Friend

The easiest way to add someone to your friends list is to do so through an XBOX 360 console. However, suppose that while attending a party you meet someone new and you want to add the person to your XBOX Live friends list right from your phone. To do so, follow these steps:

1. Press the Start button.

2. Tap the XBOX Live button.

3. Flick the screen to access the XBOX Live page.

4. Tap the Achievements link.

5. When the Achievements page loads, flick the screen to access the Friends page.

6. Tap the Find icon.

7. Enter the gamertag you want to search for.

8. When the search results are returned, look at the profile to verify that you have added the correct gamertag.

9. Tap the Add button.

10. The new gamertag is added to your friends list pending approval.

Adding a Friend

XBOX Live is set up so that no one can add you as a friend without your approval. When you add someone new to your friends list, the name is added pending approval. The next time the person you added signs into XBOX Live he or she receives a friends request in which they can approve or deny your request. That being the case, the Profile screen for your friend contains a Send icon you can use to message that friend.

Removing a Friend

You can remove another gamer from your friends list by following these steps:

1. Press the Start button.

2. Tap the XBOX Live button.

3. Flick the screen to access the XBOX Live page.

4. Tap the Achievements link.

5. When the Achievements page loads, flick the screen to access the Friends page.

6. Tap on the friend you want to remove.

7. When your friend's profile is displayed, tap the Remove icon.

8. When Windows asks you if you are sure that you want to remove the friend, tap OK.

Sending Messages to Your Friends

XBOX Live contains a messaging system that lets gamers send email messages to each other:

1. Press the Start button.

2. Tap the XBOX Live button.

3. From the Collections screen, tap the XBOX Live Extras icon.

4. When XBOX Live Extras loads, flick the screen to the Friends screen.

5. Tap on the friend to whom you want to send a message.

6. Tap the Send icon.

7. Compose your message and tap Send.

It's Not All Good

Messaging only works if you have an XBOX Live Gold subscription. Otherwise, you will not receive XBOX Live messages on your phone and will not be able to send messages to friends. Attempting to do so results in a warning message indicating that you must be an XBOX Live Gold member to send messages. If you do have an XBOX Live Gold membership and are having difficulty sending or receiving messages, be sure to check the privacy settings, which are discussed later in this chapter.

Finding a New Game

There are a number of different games available from the marketplace. You can find new games by going into the XBOX Live hub and looking at the Spotlight screen or by going to the Collection screen and tapping the Get More Games link.

Tap Get More Games to find games for your phone. ——

This is a list of the most popular games. ——

You can browse additional games by tapping More. ——

—— **You can use the Search icon to search for games.**

If you choose to use the Get More Games link, you are taken to the Games section of the Marketplace. The Games section contains several pages that list the available games in various ways (XBOX Live, New, Featured, Genres). You can flick between these pages to see the games that are listed.

The New page lists the newest games.

You also have the option of browsing the available games by category. Simply flick the screen to the left to access the Genres list. Of course if you have a specific game that you are interested in, you can always use the Search button.

You can search the marketplace for games.

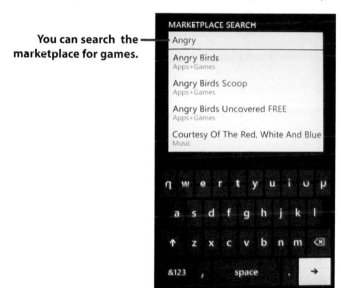

Installing a Game

When you find a game that you are interested in, you can install it by following these steps:

1. Tap the game to access the summary screen.

2. Verify the game's price.

3. Tap Show Details to get the full game description.

4. Flick the screen to the right to view screen captures and the reviews of the game. There is also a page displaying related games.

5. Tap Try.

6. When the installation process completes, the new game is listed in your game collection.

Tapping Show Details causes the game's full description to be displayed.

GAMING CONSISTENCY

As you shop for games, all of the available games are displayed in a consistent manner. Microsoft requires game developers to provide a full description and a set of screen captures for every game available in the Marketplace. There is also a free trial version of most, if not all, games. The instructions just listed demonstrate the process of downloading the trial version. When you have played the trial, there is always an option to upgrade from within the game.

Playing a Game

After you have installed a game, it is available through the XBOX Live Hub. Unlike other types of apps, XBOX games are not listed on the phone's main App List screen. To access a game, follow these steps:

1. Press the Start button.

2. Tap the XBOX Live icon.

3. Flick to the Collection screen if necessary.

4. Tap the icon for the game you want to play.

5. The game will load and you can begin to play.

Easy Access

You can pin a game to the phone's Start screen for easy access to the game. To do so, just tap and hold the game's icon and then choose the Pin to Start option from the shortcut menu.

Rating and Reviewing a Game

Just as you can read the reviews for a game, you also have the option of rating and reviewing games yourself directly through the phone. You can even rate and review the XBOX Live Essentials software if you want. To rate and review a game, follow these steps:

1. Press the Start button.

2. Tap the XDOX Live Icon.

3. Flick the screen, if necessary, to access your game collection.

4. Tap and hold the icon for the game you want to rate.

5. Choose Rate and Review from the resulting menu.

6. Assign a rating to the game by tapping a star.

7. Tap the text box and enter a review for the game.

8. Tap Submit to upload your review.

Default Games

Some Windows Phone devices list some games within the Collection by default. Often times these default games are not actually installed, but rather are simply game installation shortcuts. You can identify such a shortcut because it will include a Try Now link beneath the game's title. Default links like these also offer a Remove link rather than an Uninstall link and lack the option to rate and review the game.

Uninstalling a Game

1. Press the Start button.

2. Tap the XBOX Live icon.

3. Flick the screen if necessary to access your game collection.

4. Tap and hold the icon for the game you want to remove.

5. Tap the Uninstall option.

6. Some games are removed at this point, while others display a confirmation screen asking if you really want to remove the game.

Let's not forget that Windows Phone 7 devices can also make phone calls.

In this chapter you learn about all the different ways you can use your Windows Phone 7 as an actual phone! Make standard calls, conference calls, configure and access your voicemail, and mayb send a text or two.

8

The Phone

It is really amazing to see just how far cell phones have progressed over the years. Smart phones have become so jam-packed with features that having the ability to make a phone call has become something of an afterthought. After all, this chapter is near the end of the book, and I am just now getting around to talking about using Windows Phone devices as a phone.

Making a Phone Call

As you would probably expect, Windows Phone makes it simple to place a phone call. To do so, follow these steps:

1. Press the Start button.

2. Tap the Phone icon (Each carrier assigns a different name to this icon).

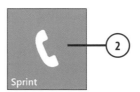

3. When you reach the Call History screen, tap the Keypad icon.

4. Dial the phone number.

5. Tap call.

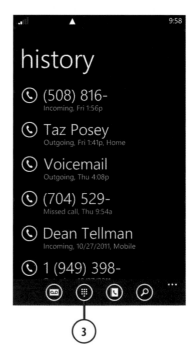

Calling Your Contacts

Windows Phone is designed so that you can access your contact list directly through the Phone app. You can call one of your contacts by following these steps:

1. Press the Start button.

2. Tap the People tile.

3. Tap the contact you want to call.

4. Tap the number you want to call.

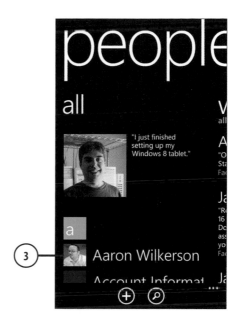

Ending a Call

When you are done with a call, you can end it by tapping the End Call button. However, if the person you are talking to hangs up first, the call is terminated automatically, and the End Call button is no longer displayed.

Tap the End Call button to terminate the call.

The Speaker Phone

Like most of the cell phones on the market, Windows Phone devices can be used as a speaker phone. To activate the speaker phone while you are on a call, follow these steps:

1. Tap the Speaker icon.

Tap the Speaker tile to use the phone as a speaker phone.

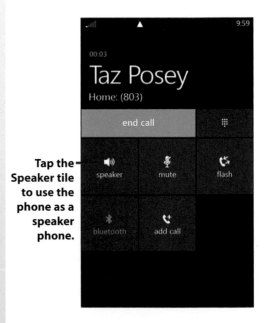

Muting a Call

If it becomes necessary to mute a call, you can do so by following these steps:

1. Tap the Mute button.

2. The Mute button is highlighted in blue to indicate that the call is muted. The Words On Mute also appear next to the timer. You can tap the Mute button again to unmute the call.

The phone indicates that the call is muted.

Tap the Mute icon to mute a call.

Accessing the Keypad

Whether you are checking your answering machine at home or calling your cellular provider with a question about your account, you are bound to occasionally run into menus that require you to press specific buttons on your keypad. If you encounter such a menu during a call, you can access the keypad by tapping the keypad icon.

During a call you can press the keypad icon to access the telephone keypad.

Missed Calls

When you miss a call, the Phone icon on the start screen displays a number reflecting the number of calls that you have missed.

If you tap the Phone icon the History screen will display all of your recent calls. Missed calls are highlighted and flagged as missed. You can return the call by tapping on the phone icon next to the missed call.

The Phone tile displays the number of calls that you have missed.

Missed calls are colored and listed as missed.

You can return a call by tapping the phone icon.

Accessing Your Voice Mail

When someone leaves you a voice message, the phone tile on the Start screen displays the voice mail icon as a way of indicating that you have a message waiting for you.

To retrieve a voice message, follow these steps:

1. Tap the Phone icon.

2. When you get to the Call History screen, tap the Voice Mail icon. This icon provides one-touch access to your voice mail.

—**This icon indicates that you have a new voice message.**

Configuring Your Voice Mail

Most cell providers design their phones to be able to access voice mail without you having to make any configuration changes. However, it is possible to manually provision your phone with a voice mail phone number. To do so, follow these steps:

1. Press the Start button.

2. Tap the Phone icon.

3. When you get to the Call History screen, flick the ... icon upward to reveal the submenu.

4. Tap Call Settings.

5. Tap the Voicemail Number field.

6. Enter your voice mail number.

7. Tap Save.

Conference Calling

Assuming that the service is offered by your cellular provider, you can use Windows Phone for conference calling. To add an additional person to a call, complete the following steps:

1. Place a call.

2. Tap Add Call.

3. Your previous call is placed on hold.

4. Use either the Keypad or the address book to place a call to the third person.

5. When the recipient answers the call, tap the Merge Calls button.

This blue box indicates that the current call is on hold. The box rotates between displaying this message and the name of the person who is on hold.

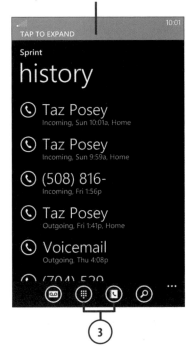

6. The phone lists the people who are participating in the conference.

6 — Taz Posey, Taz Posey

Answering a Call

When you receive a call, the device displays the caller ID information for the person who is calling, along with a picture (if you have a picture associated with the caller's contact information). You can answer the call by tapping the Answer icon.

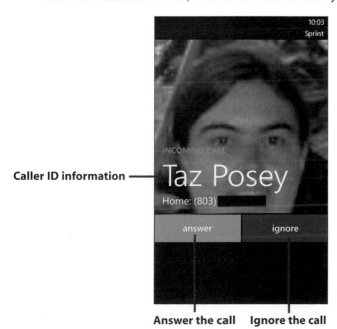

Caller ID information — Taz Posey

Answer the call   **Ignore the call**

Call Waiting

If another call comes in while you are on the phone, the device's screen displays the caller ID information for the caller. If you choose to answer the call, your original call is placed on hold. You can switch back and forth between the two calls by tapping the bar at the top of the screen.

The original call ——

The incoming call ——

Changing Ringtones

You can change the phone's ring tone by following these steps:

1. Press the Start button.

2. Flick the arrow icon to access the App list.

3. Scroll to the bottom of the App list and tap Settings.

4. Tap Ringtones + Sounds.

5. Tap the Ringtone field.

6. Sample a ringtone by tapping the Play button that's located to the left of it.

7. Tap the ringtone you want to use.

Ring and Vibrate

The Ringtones and Sounds screen contains an option to turn the ringer on and off by using a slide-bar. You can use another slidebar on this screen to turn vibration on and off.

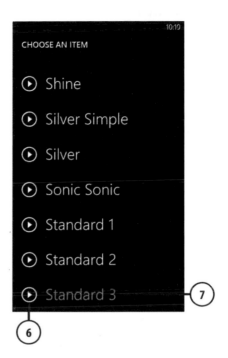

CHOOSE AN ITEM

▶ Shine

▶ Silver Simple

▶ Silver

▶ Sonic Sonic

▶ Standard 1

▶ Standard 2

▶ Standard 3 — 7

6

It's Not All Good

Microsoft has really dropped the ball when it comes to ringtones. Previous Windows phones were designed so that any .WAV file could be used as a ringtone. Sure, the operating system had default ring tones, but if you knew what you were doing, you could easily copy your own .WAV files into the ring-tones folder to make them available as a ring tone choice. I used to routinely convert MP3 or WMA files to WAV files just so that I could use them as ring tones on my phone. When I retired my last phone for example, I was using the guitar riffs from Dio's "Give Her the Gun" as my ringtone.

The original Windows Phone 7 release offered a couple dozen ringtones, but nearly all of them are variations of one single ring tone. There was no way to add your own ring tones to the phone, nor were additional ringtones available for download. You were stuck using the ringtones that Microsoft and your phone manufacturer gave you.

In Windows Phone 7.5, it is finally possible to create a custom ringtone, but the process is nonintuitive. I explain the process in the next section.

Using Custom Ringtones

Windows Phone 7.5 does allow you to create custom ringtones, but the process is not intended for beginners. If you want to use a custom ringtone, you must start by creating a sound file that will be used as the ringtone. The sound file you create must meet several criteria including

- The sound file must be in either MP3 or WMA format.

- It must be less than 1 MB in size.

- The file must not be copy protected and cannot use Digital Rights Management (DRM)

- The file must be less than 40 seconds in length.

When you have created your sound file, add it to your Zune collection. Next, follow these steps:

1. Open the Zune software.

2. Choose the Collection option.

3. Select the Music collection.

4. Scroll through the list of songs until you locate the ringtone you just created.

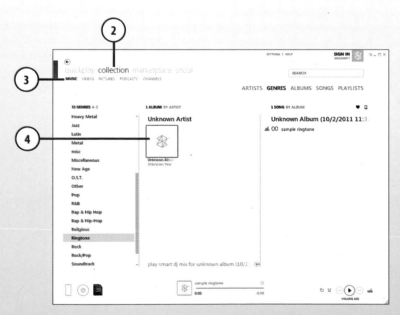

5. Right-click the ringtone and choose the Edit command from the shortcut menu.

6. Enter the word Ringtone into the Genre field. The Ringtone genre does not exist by default, so you must type it. The word Ringtone must be capitalized and spelled correctly. Using the Ringtone genre causes the sound file to be treated as a ringtone and prevents it from showing up in the phone's music collection.

7. Click OK.

8. Drag the ringtone to the Phone icon to synchronize it with your phone.

9. Press the phone's Start button.

10. Flick the screen to access App list.

11. Scroll through the App list and tap Settings.

12. Tap Ringtones + Sounds.

13. Tap the Ringtone field.

14. Select your new ringtone from the Custom section at the top of the list of available ringtones.

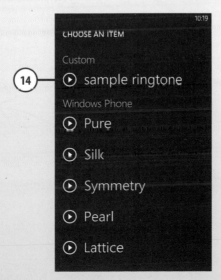

Talking Caller ID

Windows Phone 7.5 allows you to configure the phone's caller ID to verbally announce the person who is calling. When a call comes in, the ringtone initially plays at the normal volume. After a couple of seconds the ringtone volume is reduced, and the caller is announced. You can enable the talking caller ID feature by following these steps:

1. Press the phone's Start button.

2. Flick the screen to access the App list.

3. Scroll through the App list and tap Settings.

4. Tap Ease of Access.

5. Set the Speech for Phone Accessibility option to On.

Call History

The Call History screen displays your most recent phone calls along with the date and time of each call. Tapping a name within your call history list brings up the contact information for that person. Tapping the phone icon next to an item on the history list places a call to that person.

You can call someone by tapping the phone icon next to their name.

If you want to clear your call history, you can do so by flicking the … icon upward to reveal the submenu and tapping the Delete All option.

You can clear your call history by choosing the Delete All option.

International Assist

The International Assist option, which is enabled by default, is designed to automatically correct the most common errors that are made when dialing international numbers. You can enable or disable the International Assist feature by following these steps:

1. Press the Start button.
2. Tap the Phone icon.
3. From the Call History screen, flick the ... icon upward to reveal the submenu.
4. Tap Call Settings.
5. Slide the International Assist slidebar to either On or Off.

SIM Security

It's Not All Good

You should exercise extreme caution when using the SIM Security feature, as it is possible to permanently disable your SIM card, rendering it useless!

Some but not all Windows Phone devices make use of a SIM card to link the phone to the owner's account with the cell provider. Because SIM cards can be moved from one cellular device to another, it is possible to protect a SIM card with a PIN.

Enabling SIM Security

If you have a Windows Phone device that uses SIM cards, you can protect your phone against unauthorized use by enabling the SIM Security feature. To do so, follow these steps:

1. Press the Start button.

2. Tap the Phone icon.

3. From the Call History screen, flick the ... icon upward to access the submenu.

4. Tap Call Settings.

5. Set the SIM Security option to On.

The Show My Caller ID option does not exist on all phones.

You are given three attempts to enter your PIN.

How SIM Security Works

You should only enable SIM Security if you know your SIM PIN. As you can see in the figure, you only have three attempts to enter the PIN correctly.

If you enter your PIN incorrectly three times in a row, you will be locked out of the phone. The only way to regain access is to contact your cell provider and get the Service Provider Key (SPK). As you can see in the figure that follows, you have ten attempts to enter the SPK correctly.

The SIM card is locked at this point.

You have ten more attempts at unlocking the SIM card before it is permanently destroyed.

When you enter the Service Provider Key, you are prompted to provide a new SIM PIN for use with the phone. You are then asked to confirm the new PIN. At this point, the SPK is validated. If you enter the SPK incorrectly too many times, the SIM will be permanently disabled and can no longer be used with the phone.

You can't make calls if the SIM card is disabled.

When this happens, the phone acts as if a SIM is not even installed.

Soon after the SIM is permanently locked, the phone begins to have trouble.

After a few minutes, phone-related features begin to fail and remain unavailable until a new SIM is installed.

This is what happens when the SIM becomes permanently locked.

Airplane Mode

The FAA requires cell phones to be turned off during a flight. Like most other smart phones however, turning off a Windows Phone device does not disable the radio. If you want to take a Windows Phone device on an airplane, you have to put the phone into Airplane Mode (or do a full shutdown by holding down the power button and swiping the screen when prompted). Airplane Mode disables the radios used for cellular communications, Wi-Fi, and Bluetooth communications, while allowing you to continue to use the device's other features.

Enabling Airplane Mode

To put the phone into Airplane mode, follow these steps:

1. Press the device's Start button.

2. Flick the arrow icon to access the App list.

3. Scroll to the bottom of the App list and tap Settings.

4. Tap Airplane Mode.

5. Set the slidebar to the On position. An airplane icon indicates that the phone is in Airplane Mode.

Disable Airplane Mode

When you arrive at your destination, you can disable airplane mode by going back to the Airplane Mode screen and setting the slidebar to the Off position.

This icon indicates that airplane mode is enabled.

Bluetooth

Windows Phone devices can be paired with a hands free device, but the exact method required for establishing Bluetooth connectivity varies depending on the device being used.

For Windows Phone to use a Bluetooth device, it must be connected to it through a procedure known as pairing. Simple devices, such as a Bluetooth headset, can often be paired simply by pressing a button. More complex devices, such as hands-free systems that are integrated into vehicles often require you to enter a PIN into your phone before it can be paired with the vehicle. For example, you will notice that the screen in the figure that follows displays the name of my vehicle's hands free device as well as a PIN. When I paired my Windows Phone device with the vehicle, I was required to provide this PIN.

Pairing Your Phone with a Bluetooth Device

The method I used is listed here, but the actual steps you have to follow vary depending on the device you are using.

1. Put the Bluetooth device into Registration mode to begin the pairing process.

2. Press your Windows Phone device's Start button.

3. Flick the arrow icon to access the App list screen.

4. Scroll to the bottom of the App list and tap Settings.

5. Tap Bluetooth.

6. Move the slidebar to the On position. The device searches for any available Bluetooth devices.

7. When a Bluetooth device is discovered, tap on the device. The device name may initially be displayed as Headset, regardless of the type of device that you are actually connecting to. Tap on the listing for the device to begin the passing process.

If you are connecting the phone to a vehicle, make note of the pass-key.

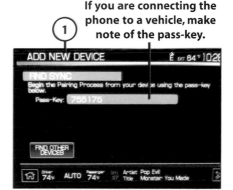

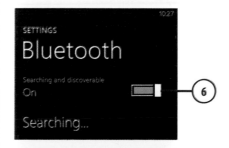

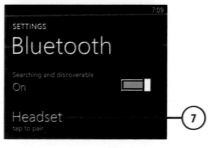

8. You might be prompted to enter a PIN. In this case, the PIN is displayed on the vehicle's screen.

9. Tap Done to complete the pairing process.

The device name now reflects the device that you are actually connecting to.

BLUETOOTH COMPATIBILITY

The functionality that can be achieved through a Bluetooth connection varies widely depending on the type of Bluetooth device being connected. In some cases though, the phone can interact with the Bluetooth device in ways you might not expect.

I own a 2011 Ford Fusion equipped with Microsoft Sync. When my Windows phone is connected to the car, the LCD display in my dash displays the current signal strength as well as the amount of battery remaining.

Perhaps the most impressive feature, however, is that I can text while I am driving! When a new text message comes in, the car reads it to me. I can verbally compose and send a response without ever taking my hands off the wheel. The speech recognition engine isn't perfect, but it seems to work pretty well, and the phone confirms what it thinks I said prior to sending the text.

SMS Text Messaging

Like any other cell phone, Windows Phone allows for the sending and receiving of SMS text messages. The Messaging tile located on the Start screen provides access to the text messaging client. This tile also displays the current number of unread text messages.

Reading a Text Message

When you receive a text message, the Messaging tile on the Start screen changes to reflect that a new message has arrived. When you tap this tile, you see all of your most recent text message conversations. The new text message is displayed at the top of the screen along with the first part of the message. This text is displayed in blue as a way of indicating that the message is new. You can read the message by tapping it.

A banner along the top of the screen displays the new text message for a few seconds.

The Messaging icon reflects the number of new text messages.

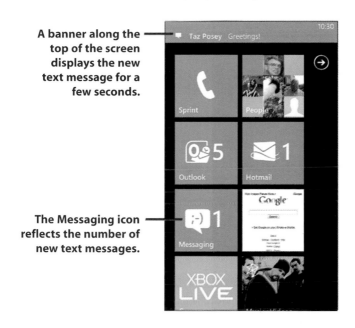

Replying to a Text Message

When you open a new text message, it is displayed in conversation view. The original message is listed within a speech bubble, and Windows places an empty speech bubble beneath the most recent message. To reply to the message, simply enter your response into this speech bubble and tap the Send icon.

The original message —

Enter your response here.

Tap here to send the response.

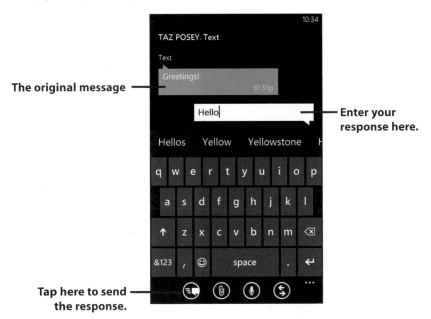

Sending a New Text Message

If you want to compose a new text message, you can do so by following these steps:

1. Press the Start button.

2. Tap the Messaging tile.

3. Tap the New icon.

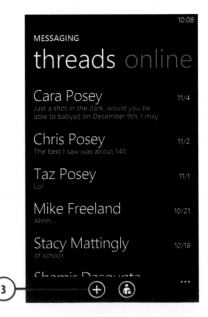

4. Enter the recipient's phone number in the To field.

5. Tap the speech bubble.

6. Enter the text you want to send.

7. Tap the Send icon.

Sending a Text Message to a Contact

If you want to send a text message to one of your contacts, you can do so by following these steps:

1. Press the Start button.

2. Tap the Messaging tile.

3. Tap the New icon.

4. Tap the + icon, located to the right of the To field.

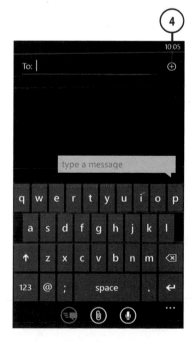

5. Tap the name of the contact to whom you want to send the message.

6. If there are multiple phone numbers listed for the contact, you are prompted to choose the number you want to send the message to.

7. Tap the speech bubble.

8. Compose your message.

9. Tap Send.

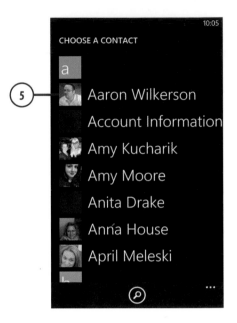

Sending a Picture Through a Text Message

If you have pictures stored on your phone, you can easily send a copy of a picture to a friend through a text message. To do so, follow these steps:

1. Press the Start button.

2. Tap the Messaging tile.

3. Tap the New icon.

4. Enter the recipient's phone number or choose a recipient from your contact list.

5. Tap the speech bubble.

6. Compose your message.

7. Tap the Attach icon.

8. Tap Camera Roll or choose one of your albums.

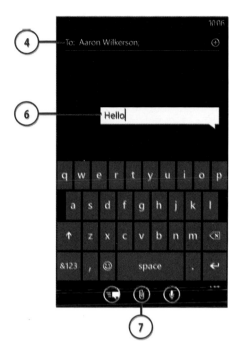

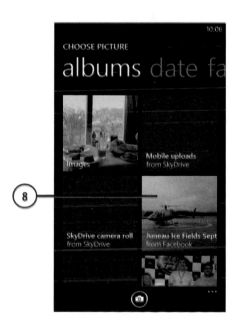

9. Tap the picture you want to send.

10. Tap Send.

**The picture is displayed
within the speech bubble.**

REJECTED PICTURES

Occasionally you might receive a notification that a picture you sent to a friend was not delivered successfully. This problem is not usually related to Windows Phone but rather to the recipient's cellular service. Some cell providers limit the size of text message attachments and might reject a message containing an image that exceeds the size limit. Pictures might also be rejected if you do not have adequate signal strength.

Go Further

Sending a Picture from the Camera

Just as you can send a friend a copy of a photo that is stored in your phone, you can also send an image directly from your phone's camera without having to first save the image to your phone. To do so, follow these steps:

1. Press the Start button.

2. Tap the Messaging tile.

3. Tap the New icon.

4. Enter the recipient's phone number or choose a recipient from your contact list.

5. Tap the speech bubble.

6. Compose your message.

7. Tap the Attach icon.

8. Tap the Camera icon.

9. Snap a picture.

10. Tap Accept.

11. Tap Send.

Removing an Image

If you change your mind about sending an Image, you can tap the Remove icon prior to sending the image. Doing so removes the picture from the message.

Text Conversations

Text messages are grouped into conversations. When you tap the Messaging tile, you will see a list of everyone you have recently had a conversation with. Each person's name is listed along with an excerpt from the most recent message in the conversation. The excerpt can be from a message that was sent to you by the person or that you sent to the person.

Each name on the list represents a separate conversation thread.

An excerpt from the most recent message in each thread is displayed beneath the name.

You can display a thread by tapping on it.

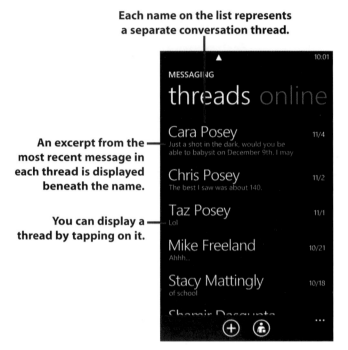

MESSAGING

threads online

Cara Posey	11/4
Just a shot in the dark, would you be able to babysit on December 9th, I may	
Chris Posey	11/2
The best I saw was about 140.	
Taz Posey	11/1
Lol	
Mike Freeland	10/21
Ahhh...	
Stacy Mattingly	10/18
of school	

10:01

You can view a conversation by tapping it. Upon doing so, Windows shows you all of the messages within the conversation. You are able to scroll through the messages by flicking the screen up or down.

When you tap on a conversation thread, Windows Phone 7 shows you all of the messages within the thread.

You are given the option of continuing the conversation.

It's Not All Good

Windows Phone groups conversations based on who the conversation was with, not on when the conversation took place. This can lead to some potentially confusing conversations. If you send a message to someone (or receive a message from someone) and a conversation already exists, the message will be added to the previously existing conversation, regardless of when the original conversation actually took place. This can lead to a bit of confusion if you go back and read a conversation later on. Thankfully, Windows does display a date and time stamp for each message.

Deleting a Message

Occasionally you might need to delete a single message without deleting an entire conversation. To do so, simply tap and hold the message you want to delete and then choose the Delete option from the resulting menu.

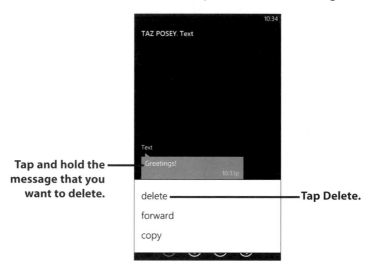

Tap and hold the message that you want to delete.

Tap Delete.

Forwarding a Message

Windows Phone gives you the ability to forward a message to someone else. To do so, tap and hold the message you want to forward and then choose the Forward option from the resulting menu. The forwarded message is displayed within a new text message. All you have to do is enter a recipient and then tap the Send icon.

Tap and hold the message that you want to forward.

Tap Forward.

Deleting a Conversation

If you want to delete an entire conversation thread, simply tap and hold
on the listing for the thread on the
Conversations screen and then
choose the Delete option from the
resulting menu.

As an alternative, you can delete a
conversation by following these
steps:

1. Tap the conversation you want to
   delete.

2. Flick the ... icon upward to reveal
   the shortcut menu.

3. Tap Delete Thread.

4. When prompted for confirmation,
   tap Delete.

Delivery Confirmation

Windows Phone provides automatic delivery confirmation for text messages. The delivery confirmation feature doesn't do anything if a message is delivered successfully, but it provides you with a warning message if delivery fails. The Delivery Confirmation feature is enabled by default, but if you need to disable it for any reason, you can do so by following these steps:

1. Press the Start button.

2. Tap the Messaging tile.

3. When you see the Conversations screen, flick the ... icon upward to reveal the submenu.

4. Tap Settings.

5. Set the SMS Delivery Confirmation slidebar to Off to disable delivery confirmation. You can re-enable delivery confirmation by setting the slidebar to On.

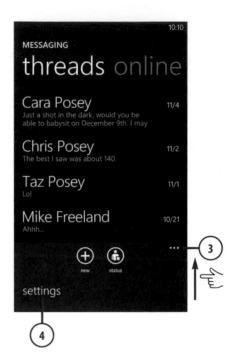

Group Text

If you are sending a text message to multiple recipients, it might be better to group all of the replies into a single conversation thread rather than grouping each person's response into a separate thread. You can accomplish this by enabling the Group Text feature. To do so, follow these steps:

1. Press the Start button.

2. Tap the Messaging tile.

3. When you see the Conversations screen, flick the ... icon upward to reveal the submenu.

4. Tap Settings.

5. Set the Group Text slidebar to On to enable the Group Text feature.

Windows Phone 7's Local Scout feature can effortlessly locate nearby restaurants.

Windows Phone 7 puts a wealth of content at your fingertips. In this chapter, you will learn how to track down whatever it is that you are looking for—whether it is stored on your phone or on the Internet.

Search

Although it might seem a bit unusual for a phone, Windows Phone 7.5 devices can accumulate a lot of data. Many devices include up to 16GB of storage, which can be used for storing apps, messages, photos, videos, music, maps, Microsoft Office documents, and more. The built-in search function can make it easy to locate specific items regardless of how much data your phone accumulates. The phone is also designed to perform Internet searches when appropriate and can even take your location into account when compiling the search results. This chapter discusses all the different ways that you can use the phone's built-in search feature.

The Search Button

As discussed in the first chapter, Windows Phone devices come equipped with a hardware search button. You can use this button to perform a search at any time, regardless of what you are doing. The Windows Phone 7 operating system is designed in a way that allows the search button to be context sensitive. In other words, what happens when you press the Search button varies depending on what you are doing at the moment. The phone attempts to perform the type of search that makes the most sense for your current situation.

The Search Button

Call History

If you tend to make or receive a lot of phone calls, it can sometimes be frustrating to try to manually scroll through your call history in search of a specific phone number. This process can be made easier by searching your call history. To perform a search, follow these steps:

1. Press the Start button.

2. Tap the Phone tile to access the Call History list.

3. Press the Search button.

4. Enter your search criteria.

The search interface allows you to search by first or last name. For example, in the figure I entered T into the search box, and the search results showed someone with a first name beginning with the letter T. The search results are displayed instantly as you type each letter of your query. There is no need to enter an entire name in most cases.

SEARCHING PHONE NUMBERS

The Call History search allows you to search phone numbers but only if a call was made to or received from someone who is not in your contacts list. For example, suppose you needed to call someone you had previously called. You remember that they are in the 803 area code, but you can't remember the phone number. In this type of situation, you could search the call history for 803. However, the search will not return any results for contacts who also happen to be in the 803 area code.

Go Further

Contact Search

You can search your contacts in much the same way that you can search your call history. The biggest difference is that when you search the call history, the only results returned are for people you have called or who have called you. Contact list searches do not filter the results based on whether or not you have talked to a person recently. You can search your contacts by following these steps:

Searching for a Contact

1. Press the Start button.

2. Tap the People tile to access the People Hub.

3. Press the Search button.

4. Enter your search criteria.

Searching Your Contacts

As was the case with the call history search, you can search your contacts by both first and last name.

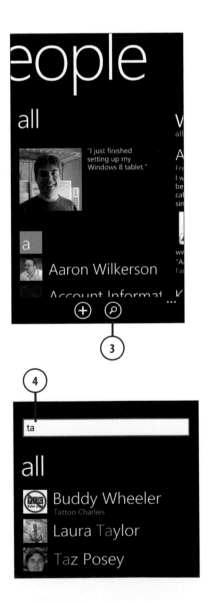

Bing Search

Although Windows Phone does have some specialized search interfaces (such as the ones used to search email or call history), pressing the Search button on the majority of the phone's screens causes the phone to open Bing. To see how a Bing search works, follow these steps:

Conducting a Bing Search

1. Press the Start button. You can actually do a Bing search from almost anywhere, but for the sake of this example, I am using the Start screen to ensure a consistent experience.

2. Press the Search button.

3. The first time you perform a Bing search, you see a screen asking if you want to allow Search to use your location. Tap Allow.

4. Enter your search criteria.

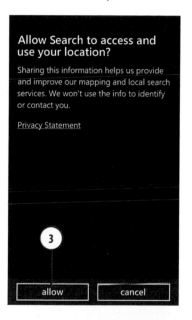

5. Bing displays search results across three different tabs. You can access the various tabs by flicking the screen to the left or to the right. The tabs include

A. **Web**—Websites related to the search phrase

B. **Local**—Relevant search results from your immediate area

C. **Images**—Images related to your search query

For example, if you were to search for the phrase Mexican Restaurants, the Web tab would probably link you to websites for the big national chains. The Local tab would show you Mexican restaurants in close proximity, and the News tab might display a story about a new Mexican restaurant that is opening up.

Searching by Voice

Although you might be inclined to enter your search criteria into the phone's search box, you can also perform verbal searches. To do so, follow these steps:

1. Press the Start button.

2. Press the Search button.

3. Press and hold the Start button.

4. Say "Find" followed by your search criteria.

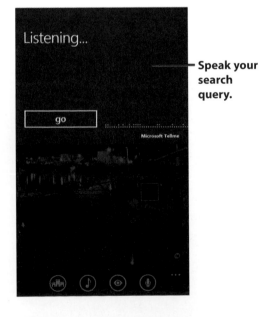

Speak your search query.

Speech Recognition

You can also interact with Windows Phone through speech recognition through a feature called Microsoft TellMe. Although not technically a search feature, Microsoft TellMe offers a convenient way to verbally interact with your phone. To access this feature:

1. Press and hold the Start button.

2. Tap Speak.

3. Speak your command.

   There are four main commands that Windows Phone understands:

   - **What Can I Say**—Causes the phone to display a few example commands. After doing so, you can tap the Speak button and then speak your command.

   - **Call**—Used to place a phone call. To use this command, combine it with a name from your contacts. For example, you could say "Call Brien Posey."

   - **Open**—Used to launch an application. An example of this command would be "Open Pac-Man."

   - **Find**—Performing a Bing search. At its simplest, you can just say "Find" followed by whatever you are looking for. For instance, you could say "Find Fast Food." If necessary however, you can also append a location such as "Find Mexican food in Redmond."

You can verbally execute a number of different commands.

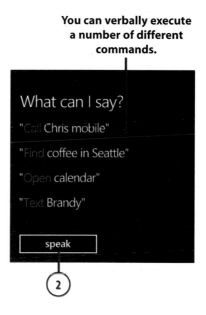

Customizing Speech Recognition

Windows Phone offers a few different options for controlling the speech recognition feature's behavior. These customizations were covered in Chapter 2, "Basic Device Settings."

Bing Music

Bing Music is a new feature that allows you to search the Marketplace for music based on a song that is playing. The phone listens to the song, identifies it, and then retrieves a listing for the song from the Marketplace. To use Bing Music, follow these steps:

1. Make sure that the music you want to sample is at an adequate volume. You can only sample the original recording. Singing or humming a song won't return a valid result.

2. Press the Search button.

3. Tap the Music icon.

4. Place the phone where it can hear the music that is playing and wait for the search results to be displayed.

This is the result of an audio search.

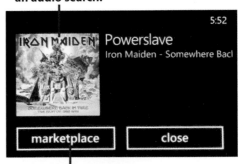

You can go directly to the item in the Marketplace.

Music History

Windows Phone 7.5 maintains a history of the music that Bing Music has identified. If you want to retrieve the list of previously identified songs, you can do so by doing the following:

1. Press the Search button.

2. Flick the ... icon upward to reveal the menu.

3. Tap the Music History option.

Occasionally Bing Music makes mistakes. This was supposed to be Keel's The Right to Rock.

These Bing Music results were correct.

Bing Vision

Bing Vision is a Windows Phone 7.5 function that allows the phone to perform searches using the phone's camera. A basic Bing Vision search can be performed against bar codes, QR codes, Microsoft tags, CD covers, DVD covers, and book covers. You can perform a Bing Vision search by completing these steps:

1. Press the Search button.

2. Tap the Vision icon.

3. Hold the phone near the item you want to search until it is displayed on screen. The phone searches for the item and returns the search results.

Bing Vision identified the album by looking at the album cover.

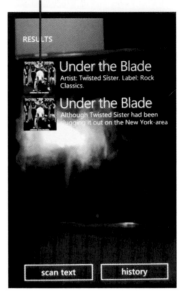

Scanning Text

In addition to being able to scan things like bar codes and album covers, Bing Vision can also scan plain text. When scanned, it is possible to search on the text or translate it to English (if the text is in a foreign language). To perform a text scan

1. Press the Search button.

2. Tap the Vision icon.

3. Hold the phone in front of the text you want to scan so the text is displayed on screen.

4. Tap Scan Text.

5. Windows draws a rectangle around the text that it identifies. Tap the rectangle containing the text you want to work with.

6. Tap either Translate or Search.

Searching with Internet Explorer

Being able to search the Internet is an important function for any smartphone. Although you can certainly use Bing for web searches, there are a number of other ways in which you can perform various types of searches through Internet Explorer.

Search Engines

Windows Phone is configured to use Bing as its search provider, and Microsoft does not give you any way of changing that. However, you still have the option of using alternative search engines such as Yahoo! and Google.

Adding a Search Engine to the Start Screen

If you tend to use a certain search engine on a regular basis, you always have the option of pinning the search engine to the Start screen. To do so, follow these steps:

1. Open Internet Explorer.

2. Go to your preferred search engine.

3. Flick the ... icon upward to reveal the submenu.

4. Tap Pin to Start.

5. The Search engine will be made available on the device's Start screen.

Even though Bing is the phone's preferred search engine, you can still use Google and other search engines.

Working with Suggested Sites

As you begin entering a URL into Internet Explorer's address bar, Bing automatically provides website suggestions as you type.

Site suggestions are enabled by default, but you can disable or re-enable this feature by following these steps:

1. Open Internet Explorer.

2. Flick the ... icon upward to reveal the submenu.

3. Tap Settings.

Bing provides suggestions as you type.

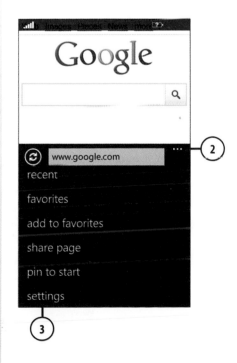

4. Use the Get Suggestions From Bing as I Type check box to enable or disable search suggestions.

④

SETTINGS

Internet Explor

Allow access to my location
On

☑ Allow cookies on my phone

☑ Get suggestions from Bing as I type

☑ Allow Internet Explorer to collect my
browsing history

Website preference
Mobile version

Open links from other apps in
The current tab

The Address Bar

The Internet Explorer address bar can be used as a search interface. If you begin typing something other than a URL, Internet Explorer pulls relevant matches from your web browsing history as well as from Bing's suggested sites. Items from your history are displayed at the top of the list.

If you enter something other than a URL, then Windows Phone 7 will treat the text as a search query and provide suggestions based on that query.

If you choose to enter a phrase into Internet Explorer's address bar rather than choosing one of the suggestions, Internet Explorer will perform a full blown Bing search on the phrase that you have entered.

Pressing Enter causes the phone to perform a full blown Bing query.

Address Mapping

In some cases, Bing is even smart enough to interpret what you have typed. For example, if you enter a street address into Internet Explorer's address bar, Bing automatically provides you with a map of the address.

If you enter a street address, Bing automatically maps the address.

Map an Address

If you want to map an address through Internet Explorer, you must enter the full address, including the city and state. Otherwise, Internet Explorer returns search results but does not map the address.

Maps

All Windows Phone devices have built-in GPS functionality. Although there are a number of built-in and third-party apps that make use of the phone's GPS, the primary application for GPS mapping is known simply as Maps. To access Maps, perform these steps:

1. Press the Start button.

2. Flick the arrow icon to access the App list.

3. Tap Maps.

4. When Windows asks you if you want to allow Maps to use your location data, tap Allow.

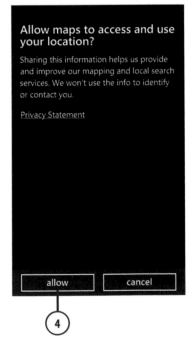

5. Maps loads and displays your current location.

The Maps interface contains several elements, including

A. Your current location

B. Scout Icon

C. Get Directions icon

D. Current Location icon

E. Search icon

Getting Directions

The Maps app is primarily designed to provide you with driving directions to a location. To get directions from your current location to a specific destination, follow these steps:

1. Press the Start button.

2. Flick the arrow icon to access the App list.

3. Tap Maps.

4. When Windows asks you if you want to allow Maps to use your location data, tap Allow.

5. Tap the Get Directions icon.

6. Enter your destination (eg: Miami, FL).

The phone calculates directions from your current location to the specified destination. Each turn on the map is marked with a number that corresponds to an instruction on a set of written directions. As you tap each step in the directions, Windows displays the corresponding location on the map.

Unlike the original Windows Phone 7 release, Windows Phone 7.5 provides verbal turn by turn directions. You can hear the latest instruction by tapping the ∧ icon.

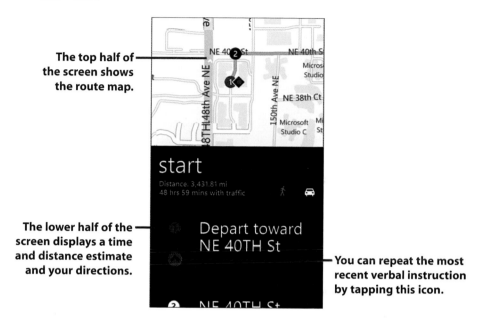

The top half of the screen shows the route map.

The lower half of the screen displays a time and distance estimate and your directions.

You can repeat the most recent verbal instruction by tapping this icon.

Clearing a Map

After you have used the phone to get directions, you might want to clear the map so that you can start fresh. You can clear the map at any time by flicking the ... icon upward and tapping Clear Map.

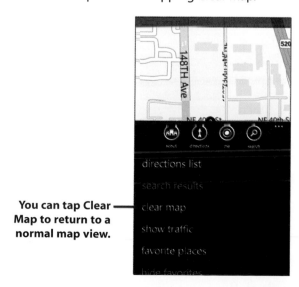

You can tap Clear Map to return to a normal map view.

Aerial View

After getting a set of directions, you can switch from Map view to Aerial view by flicking the ... icon and then tapping Aerial View On. You can switch back to map view by going to the same submenu and tapping Aerial View Off.

Aerial View overlays Aerial photos onto the map.

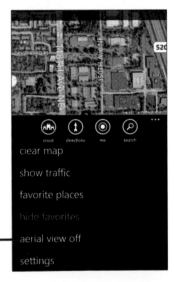

Use this option to turn Aerial View off.

Traffic

When available, Windows Phone can provide you with information about the traffic conditions along your route. When you have specified a route, you can get traffic information by flicking the ... icon and then tapping Show Traffic. Keep in mind that traffic information is only available in some areas.

Where available, the phone can display traffic information on the map.

Changing the View

By default, Maps shows a split screen view of your route. The top half of the screen shows a map; the bottom half displays driving directions. If you need to alter the view, you have a few different options, including:

A. Use the pinching gesture to zoom in and out of the map.

B. Use the flicking gesture to scroll the map in any direction.

C. Display the map full screen by tapping it.

D. You can go back to a split screen view by flicking the ... icon and choosing the Route Details option.

Finding Yourself

If you ever get lost, you can use the phone's built-in GPS functionality to determine your current location. To do so, tap the Me icon. The map scrolls to place your current location in the middle of the screen.

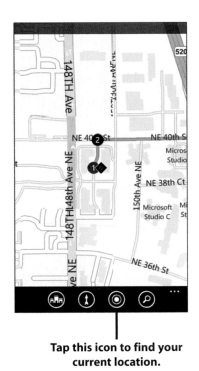

**Tap this icon to find your
current location.**

Search

At some point, you might need to search for a destination before you can ask the phone for driving directions. For instance, you might know you are supposed to meet some friends at a McDonalds in Charleston, SC, but you might not know the exact address. This is where the Search function comes into play. The phone is designed to allow you to search for geographic locations (streets, cities, and so on) or points of interest (restaurants, gas stations, stores to name a few). To perform a search, follow these steps:

Searching for a Destination

1. Press the Start button.

2. Flick the arrow icon to access the App list.

3. Tap Maps.

4. When Windows asks you if you want to allow Maps to use your location data, tap Allow.

5. Tap the Search icon.

6. Enter the name of the place you want to search for.

7. The search results will be displayed on top of the map as a series of numbered flags. Lower numbered flags represent results that are closer to your location, while higher numbers are further away.

8. Flick the ... icon upward to access the menu.

9. Tap Search Results.

10. You can tap an individual result to view it in granular detail.

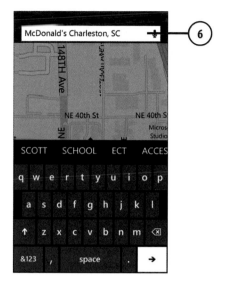

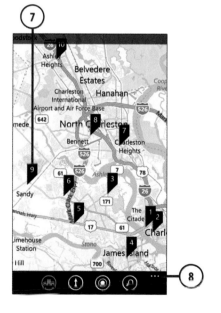

Local Scout

By far the most powerful of Windows Phone 7.5's mapping features is the Local Scout. Local Scout makes it easy to find out what else is in the area. To use Local Scout, perform a map search and choose a search result. Flip the ... icon up and tap the Scout icon.

Local Scout contains several pages, including

- **Eat+Drink**—A list of bars and restaurants in the area around your search result.

- **See+Do**—A list of attractions in the area.

- **Shop**—A list of nearby stores.

- **Highlights**—The most notable nearby locations.

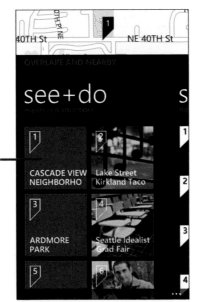

Search results are often displayed on a series of quick cards. You can tap a card to access information about the search result.

When possible, Windows Phone 7.5 displays scouting results as quick cards. A quick card is an icon representing a location. When tapped, the quick card displays information such as the address, phone number, and website for the selected search result. Depending on the individual quick card there might be one or more additional pieces of information such as

- **When**—Windows Phone 7.5 doesn't just display quick cards for locations. The local scout also returns local events such as concerts or sporting events. An event quick card contains a field that tells when the event is to take place.

- **Neighborhood**—Information about the surrounding area.

This is the name of the facility that you are viewing. In this case it is a shopping mall called Crossroads.

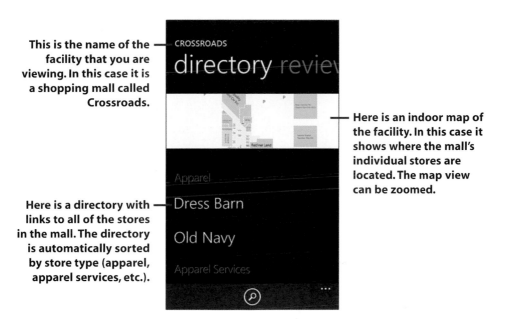

Here is an indoor map of the facility. In this case it shows where the mall's individual stores are located. The map view can be zoomed.

Here is a directory with links to all of the stores in the mall. The directory is automatically sorted by store type (apparel, apparel services, etc.).

- **Indoor Maps**—Quick cards for large public venues such as sports stadiums or shopping malls can contain indoor maps. The Indoor maps are sometimes found beneath the Neighborhood link rather than directly on the quick card.

It's Not All Good

Because Windows Phone 7.5 is so new, the amount of data returned by Local Scout varies widely depending on where you are. Last week for example, I was in Redmond, Washington (Microsoft's corporate headquarters). Local Scout performed flawlessly in Redmond. In other areas, however (even in some major cities), some of the Local Scout data does not yet exist. This is especially true for the indoor mapping feature.

Clearing Map History

If you sometimes share your phone with others, then you might wish to protect your privacy by clearing your mapping history. You can clear the map history at any time by following these steps:

1. Press the Start button.

2. Flick the arrow icon to access the App list.

3. Tap Maps.

4. When Windows asks you if you want to allow Maps to use your location data, tap Allow.

5. Flick the ... icon upward.

6. Tap Settings.

7. Tap Delete History.

8. Tap Delete.

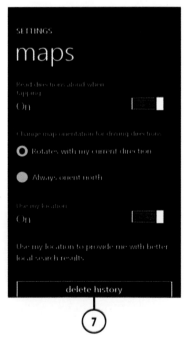

Documents

You can also use the Search button to look for One Note documents stored on your phone.

Searching for a Document

To search for a One Note document, follow these steps:

1. Press the Start button.

2. Flick the arrow icon to access the App list.

3. Tap Office.

4. When the Microsoft Office hub opens, flick the screen to either the One Note page or the Documents page.

5. Press the Search button.

6. Enter your search criteria.

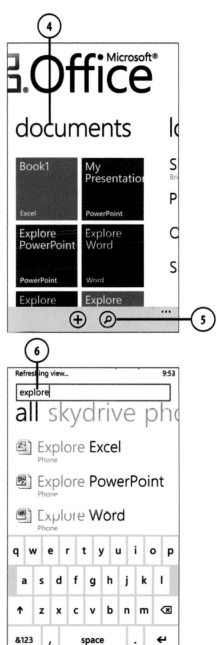

Searching Email

Windows Phone makes it easy to locate specific items within your email. To do so, follow these steps:

1. Press the Start button.

2. Tap the tile that corresponds to the email account that you want to search.

3. Tap the Search icon.

4. Enter your search criteria.

Searching Your Email

When you perform an email search, Windows Phone checks the sender line, the subject line, and the message body for occurrences of the search phrase.

Setting the Search Language

When you enter a search phrase into your phone, the phrase you enter will be searched based on the language you have configured the phone to use. If necessary, you can configure the phone to use a different language by following these steps:

1. Press the Start button.

2. Flick the arrow icon to access the App list.

3. Scroll to the bottom of the App list and tap Settings.

4. Tap Region + Language.

5. Scroll to the bottom of the Region + Language screen and tap Browser and Search Language.

6. Tap the language you want to use.

Deleting Search History

In some situations you might wish to protect your privacy by clearing your search history. You can accomplish this by following these steps:

1. Press the Start button.

2. Flick the arrow icon to access the App list.

3. Scroll to the bottom of the App list and tap Settings.

4. Flick the Settings screen to access the Applications page.

5. Tap Search.

6. Tap Delete History.

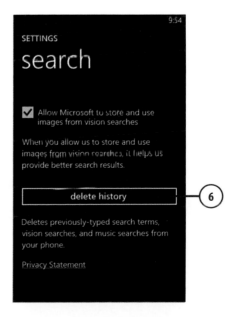

SETTINGS

region+languag

Some changes will require that you restart your phone.

1/2/2011

Long date (sample)
Sunday, January 02, 2011

First day of week
Sunday

System locale
English (United States)

Browser & search language
English (United States) — 5

9:54
SETTINGS

search

☑ Allow Microsoft to store and use images from vision searches

When you allow us to store and use images from vision searches, it helps us provide better search results.

delete history — 6

Deletes previously-typed search terms, vision searches, and music searches from your phone.

Privacy Statement

7. When prompted, tap Delete.

Are you sure?

We're about to delete all previously-typed search terms, vision searches, and music searches from your phone.

delete   cancel

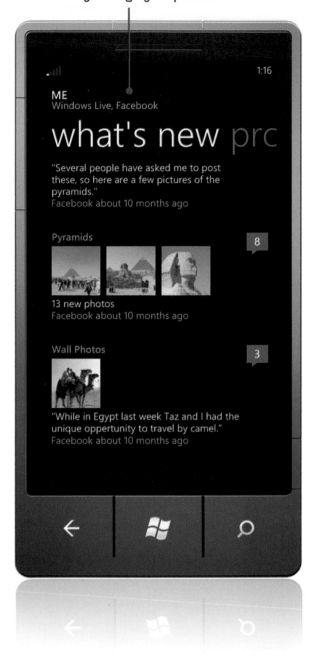

Access your Facebook account directly through your phone.

In this chapter learn how to utilize Windows Phone 7's social networking features, including the People Hub, organizing contacts, accessing Facebook, tweeting, and more.

10

Social Networking

Over the last few years, social networking has become all the rage. As such, Windows Phone was designed with social networking in mind. The phone offers native Facebook, Twitter, and LinkedIn integration so that you can access your social networks without ever having to visit the individual social networking sites. This integration allows you to interact with the various social networking sites more efficiently.

The People Hub

The People hub is Windows Phone's contact list. Unlike a normal contact list, however, the People hub displays contacts from multiple sources. For example, the People hub can simultaneously display contacts from Outlook, Hotmail, and Facebook.

The People hub contains three main screens. These screens include:

- All—The All page lists all of your contacts from all of your accounts (Windows Live, Outlook, Facebook, etc.).

- Recent—The Recent page displays contacts with whom you have recently been in contact (whether through Facebook, Outlook, or something else)

- What's New—The What's New page displays the most recent posts from your social networks.

The All Page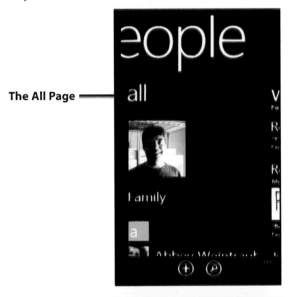

The Recent Page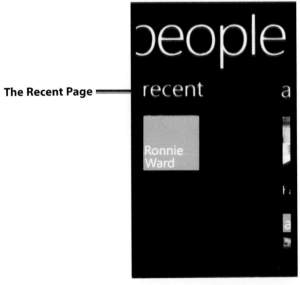

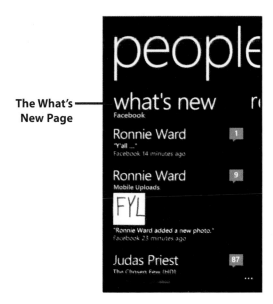

The What's New Page

Profile Information

Windows Phone displays the profile information for all of your contacts in a single place, regardless of whether the contacts are from Windows Live, Outlook, Facebook, or somewhere else. The profile information for a person contains their basic contact information, but it may also contain additional information such as their birthday or the names of their kids. As you will see later in this chapter, a profile can also act as a direct link to the person's Facebook wall.

Viewing a Profile

If you want to view the profile information for one of your contacts, you
can do so by following these steps:

1. Press the Start button.

2. Tap the People tile.

3. Scroll through the list of contacts
    until you locate the profile that
    you want to view.

4. Tap the name of the person
    whose profile you want to view.

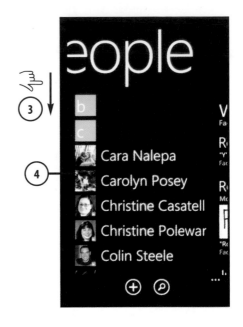

A contact's
profile

Adding a Contact

Any time you add a contact to a linked email account, that contact will automatically be synchronized to your phone. If the need should arise however, it is possible to add a contact directly to your phone. When you do, the contact that you add will also be synchronized to your mailbox. To add someone to your list of contacts, follow these steps:

1. Press the Start button.

2. Tap the People tile.

3. Flick the display to the All page.

4. Tap the + icon to add a new contact.

5. Choose the New Contact option.

6. When prompted, choose the email account that you want to add the contact to.

7. Tap the + icon next to the Name option.

8. Enter the contact's name and any other relevant information such as a nickname or the company that they work for.

9. Tap the Save icon.

10. Provide any additional profile information that you want to add, such as a phone number, an email address, or a custom ring tone.

11. When you are done, tap the Save icon.

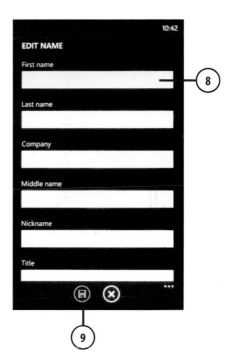

Editing a Profile

Windows Phone allows you to add or modify a contact's profile information at any time. To do so, follow these steps:

1. Press the Start button.

2. Tap the People tile.

3. Tap the name of the person whose information you want to modify.

4. Tap the Edit icon.

5. Make any desired modifications.

6. Tap the Save icon.

Information Stored in a Profile

Windows Phone allows you to add a wide variety of information to a contact's profile. The profile information is divided into categories. The following is a list of the fields that are available within each category.

Name

First name

Last name

Company

Middle name

Nickname

Title

Suffix

Phone

Phone Number

Phone Number Type (Home, Office, Mobile, etc.)

Email

    Email address

    Email address type (personal, work, etc.)

Ringtones

    Ringtone

Other

    Address

    Website

    Birthday

    Notes

    Anniversary

    Significant other

    Children

    Office Location

    Job Title

Adding Pictures

Windows Phone will automatically display profile pictures for Outlook and Facebook contacts (assuming that a profile picture exists). However, you can also add a profile picture manually. To do so, just tap the Add Photo icon when you create or edit a contact and then choose a picture from the camera roll.

MORE ON EDITING PROFILES

For the most part, the process of creating or editing contact's profiles is really straightforward. However, there are two things that you need to know. First, if you need to add any custom fields that are not available by default, you can do so by going into the Other portion of the profile and tapping Add a Field. The other thing that you need to know is that while you are free to make changes to email address profiles, you cannot make any changes to anyone's Facebook profile except for your own.

Go Further

Deleting a Contact

If you want to remove a contact from your phone, you can do so by completing the following steps:

1. Press the Start button.

2. Tap on the People tile.

3. Tap and hold the contact that you want to remove.

4. Choose the Delete option from the pop-up menu.

5. When Windows asks you if you really want to delete the contact, tap Delete.

Delete contact?

Cara Posey will be deleted from your phone and from Windows Live.

delete   cancel

5

Synchronized Deletes

When you delete a contact, the contact is also removed from any synchronized sources. For example, if you delete an Outlook contact, the contact will also be removed from the Contacts list associated with your Microsoft Exchange mailbox.

Searching for a Contact

As you begin linking multiple accounts to your phone, there is a good chance that you will accumulate a rather long list of contacts. Thankfully, you don't have to scroll through the full list of contacts every time that you need to find a specific contact. Instead, you can do a search. To search for contact, follow these steps:

1. Press the Start button.

2. Tap the People tile.

3. Tap the Search icon.

4. Enter the name that you want to search for. You can search for the first or the last name.

Finding a Contact Quickly

Another way of locating contacts quickly is to browse for contacts by using the phone's jump lists. Jump lists let you jump to a specific letter of the alphabet in the alphabetical list of contacts. To use a jump list, follow these steps:

1. Press the Start button.

2. Tap the People tile.

3. Tap a letter of the alphabet. You can tap any letter regardless of what you are searching for.

4. Tap the letter that you want to jump to.

5. Browse for the contact that you want to find.

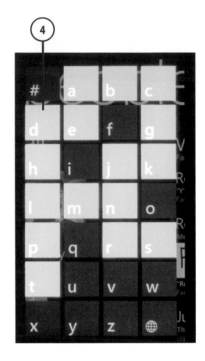

Pinning a Contact to the Start Screen

If you like to keep frequent tabs on certain friends or family members then you can pin their profile to the start screen. Doing so gives you one touch access to the person's profile so that you can easily call them, send them an email message or a text message, or view their Facebook wall. To do so, follow these steps:

1. Press the Start button.

2. Tap the People tile.

3. Tap and hold the contact whom you want to pin to the Start screen.

4. Tap Pin to Start.

Linking Contacts

Being that the People hub aggregates your contacts from multiple sources, it is possible that you may end up with multiple entries for the same person. For example, if you have a contact for the person in both your Exchange mailbox and your Hotmail box, or if you have an email and a Facebook contact for the person then you will end up with multiple contacts for the same person.

If a name appears on more than one contact list then Windows will try to automatically merge all of the profile information for that person and display it as a single contact. However, if there are inconsistencies between two listings for a contact, Windows Phone will display the contact twice.

This can be especially useful if one of your contacts gets married. She might update her Facebook profile with her married name while your Outlook contact list continues to use her maiden name. In this type of situation Windows Phone allows you to manually merge contacts by linking them together.

Merging Contacts

To merge contacts, follow these steps:

1. Press the Start button.

2. Tap the first listing for the contact that you want to link.

3. Tap the Link icon.

4. Tap the the profiles that you want to link.

5. Press the Back button.

6. Verify that the Link icon displays a number two indicating that there are two linked profiles. If necessary, you can link more than two profiles.

7. Tap the Back button and verify that there is only one listing for the linked profile.

4 ⎯

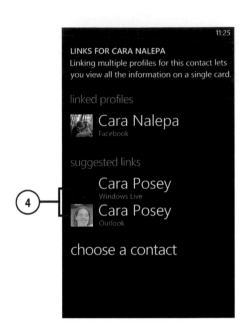

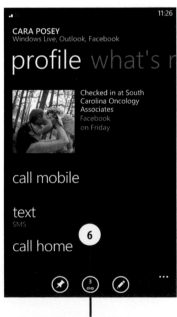

The number 3 indicates that there are three linked profiles for this contact.

Adding a New Group

Just as you can add a new contact to your phone, you can also add a new group. Groups make it easy to send a single message to multiple recipients. For instance, suppose that you frequently send email messages to several friends. Rather than manually adding each of your friends to each message that you send, you can create a group called Friends and add your friends to it. That way, you can send future email messages to the group.

1. Press the Start button.

2. Tap the People tile.

3. Flick to the All screen if necessary.

4. Tap the New icon.

5. Tap New Group.

6. When prompted, enter a name for the group that you want to create.

7. Tap Add a Contact.

8. Tap the name of a contact that you want to add to the group.

9. Tap the Save icon.

Default Group

Windows Phone automatically creates a group called Family. If you do not need this group, it can be deleted.

Changing a Group's Membership

Depending on the types of groups that you create, you may want to alter the group membership from time to time. You can accomplish this by following these steps:

1. Press the Start button.

2. Tap the People tile.

3. Flick to the All screen if necessary.

4. Tap the name of the group that you want to modify.

5. Tap the Edit icon.

6. If you want to remove someone from the group, tap on their name and then tap Remove From Group.

7. If you want to add someone to the group, Tap Add a Contact and then tap the name of the contact that you want to add to the group.

Renaming a Group

Occasionally you might create a group and then later decide that you want to call it something different. You can rename a group by following these steps:

1. Press the Start button.

2. Tap the People tile.

3. Flick to the All screen if necessary.

4. Tap the name of the group that you want to rename.

5. Tap the Edit icon.

6. Tap the Group Name field and provide a new name for the group.

Pinning a Group to the Start Screen

If you have a group that you use frequently, you may benefit from pinning the group to the Start screen. You can accomplish this task by following these steps:

1. Press the Start button.

2. Tap the People tile.

3. Flick to the All screen if necessary.

4. Tap and hold on the name of the group that you want to pin to the Start screen.

5. Tap Pin to Start.

Deleting a Group

If it becomes necessary, you can delete a group. Deleting a group only deletes the group structure—not the contacts within the group. You can delete a group by following these steps:

1. Press the Start button.

2. Tap the People tile.

3. Flick to the All screen if necessary.

4. Tap and hold the name of the group that you want to delete.

5. Tap Delete.

6. When Windows asks if you really want to delete the group, tap Delete.

Facebook Integration

Windows Phone offers built-in Facebook integration. This means that you can access your friend's Facebook walls (as well as your own) without actually having to go to the Facebook website. Instead, Facebook information is automatically made available through the People pane. Of course before you can access anyone's Facebook wall, you have to connect your phone to your Facebook account.

Connecting to Facebook

You can link your Windows Phone device directly to your Facebook account. To do so, follow these steps:

1. Press the Start button.

2. Flick the arrow icon to access the App List.

3. Scroll to the bottom of the App List screen and tap Settings.

4. Tap Email+Accounts.

5. Tap Add an Account.

6. Tap Facebook.

7. Enter your email address and password.

8. Tap Sign In.

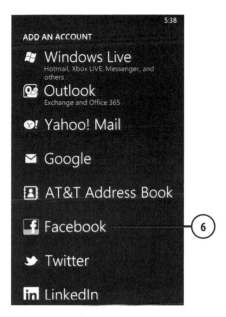

Enabling Facebook Chat

When you connect your phone to Facebook for the first time, you will see a message telling you that if you want to use your phone to chat with your Facebook friends then you will need to connect your Facebook account to your Windows Live account. You can accomplish this by tapping the Connect button.

At this point, the phone will display a screen telling you that Windows Live Messenger is requesting permission to do a number of different things (all related to Facebook). Tap the Allow icon and your Facebook account will be chat enabled.

Tap Connect to enable
Facebook chat.

Configuring Social Network Settings

The People hub provides access to a Settings page that allows you to customize your phone's behavior. Some of these settings are Facebook specific and others relate solely to the People hub. You can access these settings by following these steps:

1. Press the Start button.

2. Tap the People tile.

3. Flick the … icon upward to reveal the sub-menu.

4. Tap Settings.

The Settings screen contains a number of different settings including:

A. **Filter My Contact List**—You can tap the Filter My Contacts List button and then choose which account's contacts show up in the People hub. All contacts will remain searchable regardless of whether or not you choose to filter them.

B. **Only Show Posts From People Visible in My Contact List**—This setting can be used to prevent your profile from becoming cluttered with posts from friends of friends.

C. **Sort List By**—You can choose to sort your contacts by either first name or last name.

D. **Display Names By**—The People hub displays your contact's names in alphabetical order. This setting controls whether the list is organized according to first name or last name.

E. **Use My Location**—This setting controls whether or not your phone is allowed to use your GPS information when you check in at a location.

F. **Save Check-In History With My Windows Live ID to Improve Search Results**—You can choose whether or not Windows Live saves your check-in history.

G. **Add an Account**—You can add additional email or social networking accounts to your phone from within the Settings screen.

Viewing a Wall Post

Once you have added a Facebook account to your phone, you can access your friend's Facebook walls directly through the People hub. To view a friend's wall posts, follow these steps:

1. Tap the Start button.

2. Tap the People tile.

3. Tap on the name of a contact.

4. When the phone displays the contact's profile, flick the screen to the right to access the What's New page.

Viewing Comments to Wall Posts

Windows Phone displays a speech bubble to the right of each wall post. If the speech bubble contains a plus sign, it means that nobody has commented on the post. If you tap the + icon you can read the full post and Windows will also show you how many people like the post.

6 People like this post. —

If the speech bubble contains a number, then the number reflects the number of comments that have been made regarding the post. Tapping the speech bubble causes Windows to display the full post, the comment thread for the post, and the number of people who like the post.

12 people like this post —

— **Here are the comments for the post.**

Commenting on a Wall Post

If you want to comment on someone's Facebook wall post, then you
can do so by following these steps:

1. Tap the speech bubble next to
   the post.

2. Tap on the comment bubble.

3. Enter your comment.

4. Tap the Post icon.

Liking a Post

Windows Phone also allows you to
like someone's Facebook post. To
Like a post, follow these steps:

1. Tap on the speech bubble next to
   the post that you like.

2. Tap the Like icon.

If you accidentally like a post, you
can undo your mistake by tapping
the Unlike icon.

Writing on a Friend's Facebook Wall

Windows Phone allows you to write on a friend's Facebook wall. To do so, follow these steps:

1. Press the Start button

2. Tap the People tile.

3. Tap on the name of a contact.

4. Flick to the Profile screen if necessary.

5. Tap Write on Wall.

6. Write your post in the space provided.

7. Tap the Post icon.

8. You can go to your friend's What's New page to verify that your post was added to their wall.

Pictures in Facebook

Windows Phone allows you to view and comment on pictures that your friends have posted on Facebook. There are several different methods for viewing Facebook photos.

Viewing Individual Facebook Photos

To see the photos that your friends have uploaded to Facebook, follow these steps:

1. Press the Start button.

2. Tap the People tile.

3. Tap the name of the person whose photos you want to view.

4. Flick the screen to access the What's New page. If the person has recently uploaded any photos, they will be displayed on the What's New page as a thumbnail.

5. Tap the thumbnail for the photo that you want to view.

6. The photo is displayed along with any comments that have been made. You can also add comments of your own by using the comment box.

A larger version of the photo.

Scroll down to view the comments.

Viewing a Friend's Facebook Albums

You can also view your friend's facebook albums through Windows Phone. To do so, follow these steps:

1. Press the Start button.

2. Tap the People tile.

3. Tap on the name of the person whose albums you want to view.

4. When the person's profile is displayed, flick the screen to access the Pictures page.

5. Tap the tile representing the person's albums.

6. Tap the individual album that you want to view.

Accessing Albums from the Pictures Hub

Facebook albums are also accessible through the Pictures hub. To access Facebook albums in this way, follow these steps:

1. Press the Start button.

2. Tap the Pictures tile.

3. Tap Albums.

4. Flick the screen to access the People page.

5. Tap Choose a Contact.

6. Tap the name of the person whose albums you want to view.

Viewing All Recent Facebook Photos

Windows Phone makes it easy to view all of the pictures that have been recently uploaded by your Facebook friends. To do so, follow these steps:

1. Press the Start button.

2. Tap the Pictures tile.

3. Flick the screen to the What's New page. The What's New page displays all of the pictures that have been recently uploaded by your friends.

Missing Feature

For some reason, not all phones include the What's New page in the Pictures section.

Viewing Your Own Wall

Just as Windows Phone allows you to view your friend's Facebook walls, you can also view your own wall. To do so, follow these steps:

1. Press the Start button.

2. Tap the Me tile.

3. Flick to the What's New page to view your wall.

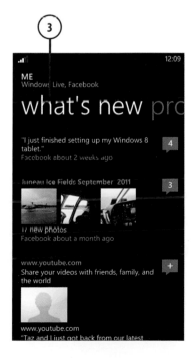

Non-Facebook Content

If Facebook is the only social network that you have configured then the What's New page will act as your Facebook wall. However, if you have accounts with Twitter and / or LinkedIn then content from those networks will also be displayed on the What's New page. If you want to view only Facebook information then tap the All Accounts link at the top of the page and then choose the Facebook option. This type of filtering will be discussed in more detail later in this chapter.

It's Not All Good

Be careful not to delete the Me tile from the Start screen. Unlike the other default Start screen tiles, there is no option to access Me from elsewhere in the Windows Phone operating system. If the Me tile is deleted, the only way to get it back is to remove your Facebook account from the phone and then add it back.

Posting Status Updates

You can perform a Facebook status update directly from your phone. To do so, follow these steps:

1. Press the Start button.

2. Tap the Me tile.

3. Flick the screen to the Profile page if necessary.

4. Tap the Post a Message link.

5. Choose whether the status update will be posted to Facebook, Windows Live, or both.

6. Type your message.

7. Tap the Post icon.

Checking In

Windows Phone also allows you to check in at a location. To perform a Facebook check-in, follow these steps:

1. Press the Start button.

2. Tap the Me tile.

3. Tap Check-In.

4. When the phone asks if it is OK to use your location, tap Allow.

5. Windows will use your location information to retrieve a list of nearby locations. Tap your desired location.

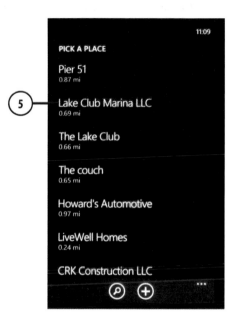

Custom Locations

Although being able to choose from a list of locations is handy, it may not work so well in dense urban areas. If you find that your location isn't on the list (or if the list is too long to sort through) you can use a different method. There are two icons at the bottom of the locations list. One is a search icon, which lets you search the locations for the one that you want to check in at. The other is an Add icon which lets you define your own locations.

Uploading a Photo

Windows Phone allows you to upload a photo from your photo roll directly to Facebook. To do so, follow these steps:

1. Snap the photo using the phone's camera if necessary. You can also upload a picture that is already in your photo roll. If you need help with using the camera, then check out Chapter 5, "Windows Phone 7 Apps."

2. Press the Start button.

3. Tap the Pictures tile.

4. Locate the picture that you want to upload.

5. Flick the … icon upward to access the sub-menu.

6. Tap Share on Facebook.

7. Enter a caption for your picture.

8. Tap the Upload icon.

>>> Go Further

FACEBOOK TAGGING

When you get ready to upload a photo to Facebook, it is possible to tag the people shown in the photo. If the photo contains one or more people, the phone will automatically draw a rectangle around each face. Just beneath the rectangle is a tag that says Who's This. If you tap on this tag you are given the choice of either typing a name or selecting a name from your Facebook contacts.

Every once in a while, Windows Phone devices may not properly detect that there are faces shown in a photo. In this type of situation you can tap the Add Tag icon and then tap the face in the photo. Windows will then allow you to either manually enter a name or choose a name from your Facebook contacts.

Facebook Chat

Windows Phone devices allow you to chat with your Facebook friends directly through your phone. To do so, follow these steps:

1. Press the Start button.

2. Tap the Messaging tile.

3. Flick the screen to access the Online page.

4. If this is the first time that you have attempted a Facebook chat from your phone you will see a message telling you that you must tap the screen to set your chat status and to see who is online. Tap on the screen to continue.

5. Set your chat status. When you do, Windows will check to see who is online.

6. At this point the phone will show you who is online. Tap the person with whom you wish to chat.

7. Enter your message.

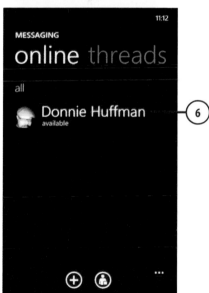

It's Not All Good

Windows Phone can take quite a while to figure out who is available for a Facebook chat. As such, the list of who is online isn't always accurate. Furthermore, Windows can take a while to add all of your Facebook friends to your contacts. If one of your Facebook friends tries to initiate a conversation before that person has been added to your contacts, the message will appear to have come from "Facebook User."

Setting Your Chat Status

You can manually set your chat status at any time by following these steps:

1. Press the Start button.

2. Tap the Messaging icon.

3. Tap the Status icon.

4. Tap your desired status.

The statuses that you can choose from include:

- Available
- Busy
- Away
- Appear Offline
- Offline

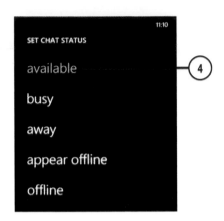

11:10

SET CHAT STATUS

available — 4

busy

away

appear offline

offline

Chatting with Facebook Friends

Facebook chats occur through the Messaging hub. You can use the Messaging hub for Facebook, SMS, and Microsoft Live chats. If a friend signs out of Facebook then the phone will attempt to automatically continue the conversation through another chat service.

When someone on Facebook initiates a chat, the message is displayed through the Messaging hub, just as an SMS text message would be.

Go Further

THE FACEBOOK APP

By now you have probably noticed that various Facebook elements are scattered throughout the phone. Wall posts are in the People hub, chat is in the Messaging area, and photos can be accessed through the Pictures hub. If you prefer to have everything in one place, then there is a free Facebook app for Windows Phone. This app, which can be downloaded through the Marketplace, allows you to access your Facebook account through a single interface.

Twitter

Windows Phone devices include full twitter integration. As such you can send and receive tweets directly through the phone without installing any extra software.

Configuring Your Twitter Account

Before you can use Twitter from your phone, you must link the phone to your twitter account. You can do so by following these steps:

1. Press the Start button.

2. Flick the screen to access the app list.

3. Tap Settings.

4. Tap Email+Accounts.

5. Tap Add an Account.

6. Tap Twitter.

7. You will now see a message indicating that Twitter must be linked to your Windows Live account. To do so, tap Connect.

8. When prompted, enter the email address and password for your Twitter account.

9. Tap Authorize App.

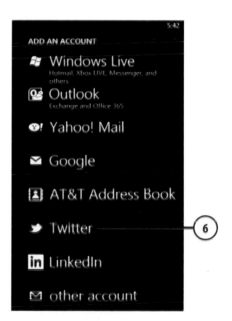

Sending a Tweet

Sending a tweet is done in essentially the same way as posting a message to Facebook. However, you must remember that tweets must be 140 characters or less in length. You can send a tweet by following these steps:

1. Press the Start button.

2. Tap the Me tile.

3. Tap Post a Message.

4. Tap the Post To field.

5. Clear all of the check boxes except for the Twitter box.

6. Tap the Done icon.

7. Enter your message.

8. Tap the Post icon.

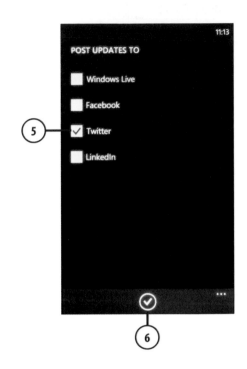

Checking Your Tweets

You can access your tweets by following these steps:

1. Press the Start button.

2. Tap the People tile.

3. Flick the screen to access the What's New page.

These feeds are coming from Twitter.

Responding to a Tweet

If you want to respond to a tweet, you can do so by following these steps:

1. Press the Start button

2. Tap the People tile.

3. Flick the screen to access the What's New page.

4. Tap on the tweet that you want to respond to.

5. Enter your comment.

6. Tap the Post icon.

Retweeting

If you see a tweet that you particularly like, you can retweet it. To do so, follow these steps:

1. Press the Start button.

2. Tap the People tile.

3. Flick the screen to access the What's New page.

4. Tap on the tweet that you want to retweet.

5. Tap the Retweet icon.

6. Tap the Retweet button.

LinkedIn

Windows Phone devices are capable of connecting to LinkedIn without the aide of any additional software. To connect a phone to LinkedIn, follow these steps:

1. Press the Start button.

2. Flick the screen to access the app list.

3. Tap Settings.

4. Tap Email+Accounts.

5. Tap Add an Account.

6. Tap LinkedIn.

7. You should now see a message telling you that you must connect your LinkedIn account to your Windows Live account. Tap Connect to continue.

8. Enter the email address and password that are connected to your LinkedIn account.

9. Tap OK, I'll Allow It.

10. Tap Continue.

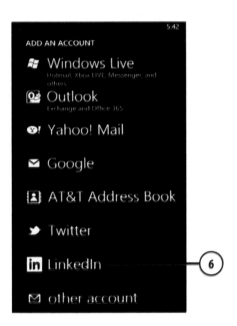

Accessing LinkedIn Content

Content from LinkedIn is shown in the same place as Facebook and Twitter content. You can view content from LinkedIn by following these steps:

1. Press the Start button.

2. Tap the People tile.

3. Flick the screen to access the What's New page.

These feeds are coming from LinkedIn.

Responding to a LinkedIn Post

You can respond to a LinkedIn post by following these steps:

1. Go to the What's New page.

2. Tap the post that you want to respond to.

3. Enter your response into the Add a Comment field.

4. Tap the Post icon.

Posting a Message

You can post a message to LinkedIn by following these steps:

1. Press the Start button.

2. Tap the Me tile.

3. Tap Post a Message.

4. Tap the Post To field.

5. Clear all of the check boxes except for the LinkedIn box.

6. Tap the Done icon.

7. Enter your message.

8. Tap the Post icon.

The Feeds Filter

Because Windows Live, Facebook, Twitter, and LinkedIn content is all aggre-gated and displayed on the What's New page, you may find that the page becomes so cluttered that it becomes difficult to find what you are looking for. If this happens, you can use the Feeds Filter to cut through the clutter.

When you access the What's New page there is a link at the top called All Accounts. This means that you are currently viewing content from all of your social networking accounts. If you tap this link you can choose an individual account. For example, you can choose to view content only from Twitter. Upon doing so, the All Accounts link changes to reflect the name of the account that you are using. That way you can tell at a glance that you are viewing Twitter content. To look at a different account (or all of the accounts), just tap the link again and choose the account that you want to view.

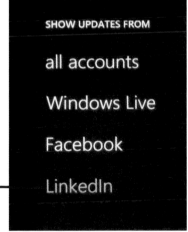

The Feeds Filter allows you to control which feeds are displayed.

The Me Tile

At first glance there doesn't seem to be anything interesting about the Me tile. It rotates between displaying your picture and the word Me. However, the tile sometimes displays notifications (on the tile itself) to show you what is going on with your social networks.

The Me tile displays notification information.

Notifications

It can be tough to keep up with what's going on with all of your social networks, especially if you use more than one. This is where the Notifications page comes into play. The Notifications page lets you know about things that are going on with your social networks. For example, if someone sends you a message or responds to your Facebook post then you will see linked notification on the Notifications page. This link summarizes the notification and you can tap the link to access the actual message or post.

You can access your notifications by following these steps:

1. Press the Start button.

2. Tap the Me tile.

3. Flick the screen to access the Notifications page.

Index

U

V

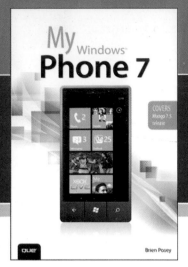

My Windows
Phone 7

COVERS
Mango 7.5
release

FREE
Online Edition

Safari.
Books Online

QUE

Brien Posey

Your purchase of *My Windows Phone 7* includes access to a free online edition for 45 days through the **Safari Books Online** subscription service. Nearly every Que book is available online through **Safari Books Online**, along with thousands of books and videos from publishers such as Addison-Wesley Professional, Cisco Press, Exam Cram, IBM Press, O'Reilly Media, Prentice Hall, Sams, and VMware Press.

Safari Books Online is a digital library providing searchable, on-demand access to thousands of technology, digital media, and professional development books and videos from leading publishers. With one monthly or yearly subscription price, you get unlimited access to learning tools and information on topics including mobile app and software development, tips and tricks on using your favorite gadgets, networking, project management, graphic design, and much more.

Activate your FREE Online Edition at
informit.com/safarifree

STEP 1: Enter the coupon code: JSARWBI.

STEP 2: New Safari users, complete the brief registration form.
Safari subscribers, just log in.

If you have difficulty registering on Safari or accessing the online edition,
please e-mail customer-service@safaribooksonline.com

  Addison Wesley   Adobe Press   ALPHA   Cisco Press   FT Press IBM Press Microsoft Press New Riders   O'REILLY

  Peachpit Press   PRENTICE HALL   QUE Redbooks   SAMS   SAS Publishing   vmware PRESS   WILEY   wrox